C000180372

and Races
in Scotland

Thanks to Andy and Hilary Spenceley, Jon Ascroft,
Lucy Colquhoun, Nigel Rose, Ross Bannerman,
Chris Upson, Scottish Hill Runners and all the race
organisers, and everyone else who helped out with
many questions and requests for information.

Special thanks to Ian and Anne Nimmo, Alan
Young and the other photographers who gave us
permission to use their pictures in this book and
to Keith Jeffrey for his patience!

Some of the historical information was derived
from *Race You to the Top* by Suse Coon.

The author and publisher have made every effort to ensure that the information in this publication is accurate, and accept no responsibility whatsoever for any loss, injury or inconvenience experienced by any person or persons whilst using this book.

published by
pocket mountains ltd
6 Church Wynd, Bo'ness EH51 0AN
pocketmountains.com

ISBN: 978-1-907025-06-8

Printed in Poland

On the Pentland skyline (pic: Alan Young) ▶

Introduction

This guide contains 35 hill-running and 35 hill-racing routes from all over Scotland. The routes are grouped into seven regions, each containing 10 classic routes, with the runs marked in green and races in red. Each chapter begins with a couple of short, straightforward routes, then builds up through slightly tougher routes lasting an hour or two and ends with long, challenging routes taking several hours to complete.

Included with every route is a map showing the basic outline of the course, along with some key details. These maps are not designed for specific navigation, and you should take the relevant OS map, along with a compass – and the ability to use both. Other summary information at the start of each route includes the distance, ascent and time taken to run the course. Everyone runs at a different pace, weather conditions change and terrain varies; however, to give a general guide, hill-run times are based on an average speed of 10km per hour, plus one hour for every 1000m of height climbed, with extra time built in for longer routes where a slower pace is often required to last the course. All times are checked against actual experience. Race pages include the race category (see p8), records (correct at September 2009), the organising club's website and other key notes.

All of the routes here have been chosen because they represent the best of Scotland's hill running, but the list contained in this guide is far from definitive. I have tried to include routes that are 'runnable' – terrain that permits running at speed, preferably on paths or grass-covered hill crests. Many of the routes are also situated in stunning locations. Some of the races have been selected to offer an ideal introduction to hill racing, others are popular events in the race calendar, and there are also longer races that present even the most experienced competitor with a challenge. Hopefully, I've also managed to throw in a few surprises!

Starting hill running

Hill running is great fun and a way to see more countryside without the need for long days out backpacking. Hill racing is all that, as well as being sociable and competitive. Both are an excellent way to keep fit. Hill running is not an expensive sport to get into, and just about anyone can take it up. Below is a guide to get you started.

Footwear The first and most important bit of gear you need to consider is footwear. Hill runners use fell shoes, designed to cope with the inevitable wet feet by allowing water in but also expelling it. They have great grip and contact at the same time as being light and durable. There is a growing choice of styles, with more manufacturers entering

the market, so think of the terrain you'll be crossing and choose to your needs. Some have excellent grip on mud, whereas others are designed with more support or sturdier soles to cope better with rock, trails or road. Fell shoes tend to have little in the way of ankle support and if you're coming from a hillwalking background, in particular, this will take some getting used to, but once you've adjusted, you'll never go back!

Clothing You're going to sweat, particularly on the uphills, then possibly have a cold wind on the crests and downhills, so tight-fitting, breathable tops are best. They take away the moisture and keep you dry. Shorts or lycra? – it's a personal choice, but lycra will protect your backside better on the inevitable fall on heather. In winter, running 'longs' or tracksters will probably be needed. Avoid hillwalking socks as they are more likely to stay wet and give blisters. Instead, try running socks; there are even pairs designed specifically for hill running. Lightweight, waterproof top and bottoms should always be carried, even in warm conditions, as an injury situation could be made considerably worse by hypothermia. A survival bag, whistle and mobile phone are pieces of kit that you will hopefully never need, but for the minimal space they take up and value in the event of an emergency they are essential. Remember, a mobile phone may not work on the hills or in the glens.

Food and drink While exercising, keep hydrated and on longer runs, carry fluid and eat something every half hour or so. You might just want to consume chocolate or jellybabies, but there are lots of specialised high-carb gels and bars available which some runners swear by, although others find them sticky and mouth-drying. In the end, it's all down to what works for you – one runner at the top of her game tells me that Marmite sandwiches are the food of the gods!

Carrying Next, you'll need something to carry your waterproofs, food, map, compass, phone, sunscreen and other stuff. A short race will require minimal baggage, so it can all be stuffed into a lightweight bum-bag. Slightly longer routes may necessitate the carrying of more provisions, so a Camelbak or OMM pack would be better suited. On routes taking several hours, or in winter, you'll need to take hat, gloves, fleece and more, so one of the larger running backpacks is ideal, but don't just opt for a hillwalking

◂ On the Two Breweries (pic: Alan Young)

rucksack. As hill running becomes increasingly popular, more space is being made available for the gear in running and outdoor shops. You might find the available choice quite daunting; however, shop staff are usually knowledgeable, so it pays to ask for their advice. Well-known hill-running brands include Walsh, Inov-8, Ronhill and OMM, with other brands like Lowe Alpine, Adidas and Salomon also designing quality hill-running gear.

Technique Once you've got the gear sorted, try out some of the shorter and easier to navigate routes at the beginning of the chapters and build up your confidence and experience. To run uphill, try to keep fairly upright on a short stride. As the ascent steepens, your speed will slow to a fast walking pace, perhaps with

hands on waist. On even steeper ascents, hunch over, put your hands onto your thighs and push to get extra drive uphill.

Along crests and plateaux, the terrain on most of the routes offers a mixture of fast running on paths and grass, bounding over heather and short strides negotiating rocks and boulders. A compromise between watching the placement of your feet and admiring the views is needed.

Downhill running takes practice – don't focus on your feet; instead, set your sights a few paces ahead and keep your arms slightly up or out to aid balance. Downhill speed is controlled by leaning your upper body – forward to speed up, back to slow down. The fastest downhill runners talk about putting their brain into neutral and just letting go

◄ Heading up Stuc a'Chroin in April

– fine on a race, but not a good idea in wild, remote areas while on your own. It's a good idea to join a hill-running club. A few are mentioned in this book, but there are many more all over the country. Clubs are sociable, organise training sessions, host runs and other events and contain like-minded folk with a wealth of experience that they are always willing to share.

Try hill racing

Hill racing is great fun, very sociable and, of course, competitive. Anyone can take part in the races listed in this guide; you don't even have to be attached to a running club (except for the Ben Nevis Hill Race). Check out the Scottish Hill Runners and Scottish Hill Racing websites for a calendar of events. Apart from a few races, you can just turn up at the event and take part. Entry fees tend to be only a few pounds and a few are free. A number of races start in forests, so anti-midge cream is recommended. It's worth turning up at least half an hour before the race is scheduled to start, which will give you time to register and chat to some of the other runners, picking up tips on the route. Prior to the race, some runners have a jog to loosen up muscles, while others prefer a few minutes stretching. On shorter races,

have a stretch and jog after the event, but on longer races, save it for later to allow time for the body to repair tiny muscle tears. Hill-racing injuries are rare and tend to be minor; however, hypothermia is an issue, so always carry at least the minimum amount of gear as specified by the organiser. Marshals may well check gear prior to the race and disqualify those breaking the rules. Marshals will also be at key checkpoints on the race (though you should not rely on their presence) and someone will 'sweep' to make sure everyone finishes. If you have to pull out of the race, always report to a marshal or the finish, as all runners must be accounted for at the end of a race. It is important to note that although many races are partially flagged and marshalled, this is primarily to direct runners where environmental or other access restrictions apply and should never be relied upon as a substitute for navigation skills. Bearing in mind that visibility in bad weather can be drastically reduced, you should not rely on markings to guide your way, particularly on high ground. Runners are ultimately responsible for their own safety on a race.

You'll notice in the summary information on each route that a category has been given to the race

– for example, AM. The first letter in the category corresponds to the ratio of climb related to distance:

A 250ft per mile and less than 20% on road
B 125ft per mile and less than 30% on road
C 100ft per mile and less than 40% on road

The second letter corresponds to the length of the race :

L long, 12 miles or over
M medium, 6 to 12 miles
S short, less than 6 miles

These categories not only give an idea of the type and length of a race, but they are also used by organisers to stipulate the gear to be worn or carried by runners. In all AL and AM races, full body cover, map, whistle and compass must be carried (as well as emergency food in AL races). Race organisers are obliged to do a kit check. You have to be over 18 to run in any race longer than 10km. Race organisers may also insist on experience, or may change the route at short notice due to weather or other circumstances beyond their control (race routes can sometimes vary from year to year too), so check the relevant website for details.

Hill safety

A number of routes in this guide venture into remote terrain and, even in summer, the weather in these hills can deteriorate suddenly,

Navigation
Hill runners need to develop map-reading and navigation skills: a good place to start is with Martin Bagness' short e-book 'Mountain Navigation for Runners', available from www.lakesrunner.com. Your local outdoors shop should also be able to offer advice about courses in your area.

changing a straightforward run into one that requires all your navigation skills. As well as carrying the minimum gear, OS map and compass recommended above, it is always advisable to let someone know your route in advance and to consider running in pairs or as part of a group. Hill running in winter brings its own set of challenges, and it is important to be certain you can complete your route within more limited daylight hours.

Access and transport

In recent years the access laws in Scotland have been reformed and in its most basic form, you have the right to access most land, providing that you do so responsibly! There are certain times of the year when some areas are particularly sensitive. Lambing takes place in March and April, bird nesting during April to July and deer-stalking from August to late October. Check the Scottish Outdoor Access Code before you go (outdooraccess-scotland.com). Scottish Natural Heritage co-ordinates the Hillphones service, which you can access to find out where stalking is taking place (snh.org.uk/hillphones).

Where possible, public transport options have been highlighted, though readers will appreciate this

Useful websites

Scottish Hill Racing
www.scottishhillracing.co.uk

Scottish Hill Runners
www.shr.uk.com

The Fell Runners Association
www.fellrunner.org.uk

Mountaineering Council of Scotland
www.mcofs.org.uk

Scottish Natural Heritage Hillphones
www.snh.org.uk/hillphones

is just not practical in many of these locations. A small selection of the routes are linear, where transport needs to be arranged to avoid a long run back. In these cases, the routes were just too spectacular to exclude and, as several end at pubs, they will hopefully provide an excuse to gather a few friends for a social after the run.

GPX files

If you have a GPS unit or mapping software, such as Memory-Map or Anquet Maps, you can obtain GPX files of the routes in this guide. These can be downloaded at:
www.stevenfallon.co.uk/
pocketmountains.html

South of Scotland's populated Central Belt and stretching away to the Borders and Galloway, the rolling green hills of the Southern Uplands provide some of the best hill running in the country. Both the Meldons and Peebles' Gypsy Glen give a fine introduction to hill running, whilst Screel provides a transition to more technical routes. More than 500 runners try to secure a place in the well-organised and marshalled Carnethy 5 Hill Race, which contrasts with the low-key and relaxed Yetholm Hill Race. Paths and fencelines aid navigation and encourage fast running over the pleasant, grass-covered Culter and Lowther Hills. The Pentland Skyline and Two Breweries events are among the most challenging hill races in the calendar, each with several peaks to climb and descend over a variety of terrain.

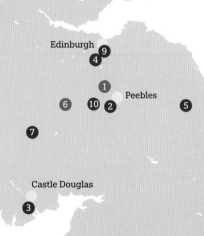

Southern Uplands

Meldon Hillforts

Distance **6.5km** Ascent **500m** Time **allow 1h15** Map **OS Landranger 73**

**Running over grassy terrain for
most of the route with occasional
bounding through ferns and heather,
this route is a fine introduction to
hill running.**

Some 4km west of Peebles, a
narrow road winds its way uphill by
Meldon Burn. There's a parking area
with noticeboard and picnic tables
1.5km up the road and it is from here
that this fine little route starts. Cross
the fence, then jump the burn and
look for one of several faint sheep
trods heading northeast by Meldon
Burn. The trails wind their way

through heather and ferns to a
walled clearing, where you'll usually
find livestock grazing. At the
northern end of this, a gate marks an
exit, where a track of sorts leads
uphill. This indistinct track makes for
swift progress as it climbs to White
Meldon's summit. A trig point stands
on the summit with the remains of
an ancient burial cairn and fort.
About turn and follow vague paths
southwards through the heather to
meet a track crossing the col. Pick up
the obvious path aiming south and
following the hill's crest. Only a small

◀ White Meldon from the southwest

pile of stones resting on the broad, flat top of South Hill Head marks the summit. Turn west and bound downhill over heather, ferns and rush-grass back to the picnic area. Cross the road and, on your right, go through a gate into a field. Keeping the wall on your left, head up to another gate, beyond which you cross the burn and meet another gate. Through this gate, aim uphill along the edge of the field, keeping the wall on your right to find a fourth gate. A path is picked up after this gate, which rises directly uphill along the edge of a forest. A minor summit is attained, with Black Meldon's fort but a brief jog away. To return, bear south and descend on pleasant grassy terrain, avoiding the many rabbits scurrying in and out of their warrens.

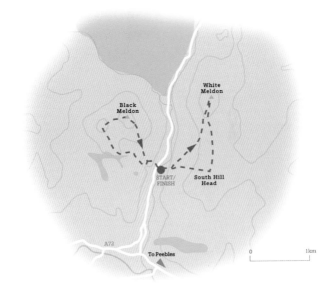

Gypsy Glen Hill Race

Distance 8.5km Ascent 300m Category BS Records 33:17 – Euan Jardine (2006), 36:28 – Susan Ridley (2008) Time of year mid-May
Map OS Landranger 73 Website www.moorfootrunners.co.uk

An excellent introduction to hill racing, this one has a bit of everything – road, grassy tracks, heather trods, a few steep rock and boulder sections, and fine views – as well as being well organised.

Starting from the south bank of the Tweed by Peebles' Tweed Bridge, the race heads southeast along Springhill Road and continues to the end of Glen Road after a gradual climb of 1.5km. It then follows the remains of the old Yarrow Valley drove road. After crossing a burn, the route climbs rough ground, exits the forest and continues to rise on a path which shadows a wall over open hillside. Further up, through a gate, the route breaks off the main path to

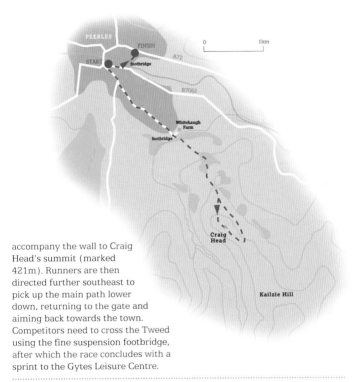

accompany the wall to Craig Head's summit (marked 421m). Runners are then directed further southeast to pick up the main path lower down, returning to the gate and aiming back towards the town. Competitors need to cross the Tweed using the fine suspension footbridge, after which the race concludes with a sprint to the Gytes Leisure Centre.

Run by the local community council as part of their 'Health Week', and with much assistance from Moorfoot Runners, the Gypsy Glen Race now regularly attracts around 50 to 60 runners. The race has been taking place for many years and has had its share of ups and downs. Its lowest point was in torrential rain in the mid-1990s when only two runners turned up – being runners of very different abilities, there was no formal contest required and they decided to go to the pub instead!

◀ Race leaders descending Craig Head

Screel Hill Race

Distance 6km Ascent 425m Category AS Records 27:32 – Gary Devine (1995), 32:37 – Trish Calder (1990) Time of year mid-April Map OS Landranger 84

Short, steep and technical, the Screel Hill Race makes the transition from Gypsy Glen's gentle hill-racing introduction to something much more serious. The real difficulty is keeping upright while attempting to avoid the rocks and tree roots on the fast descent. Do this route as a walk and you'll have time to appreciate the breathtaking views.

Just off the A711, 8km south of Dalbeattie are some tracks and walking trails heading into the woods. There is a parking area for a few cars at the foot of the trails, and this is where the informal race registration and race start take place.

Initially on a fine gravel-covered track, the race route winds its way up a gradual incline through the forest to more open felled ground. The track comes to a junction, but the race route takes neither turning and instead heads around a wall, then on a path, aiming directly uphill over uneven and rutted ground. Another track is met, but again the race heads directly uphill and into thick forest. Terrain is testing, steep and occasionally wet, and runners not only have to watch their feet but also look out for stray branches at face height! Out of the forest, the route continues uphill on a path,

◀ The Screel Hill Race begins on forest tracks (pic: Keith Jeffrey)

bypassing Screel's eastern tops above. The path crosses the summit crest through heather and arrives on the main summit, where competitors are directed westwards downhill and back into the forest. Heading eastwards and dropping height through the forest, the route makes a sudden change of direction and runners clamber back uphill, clutching at clumps of grass to emerge out of the forest just before the eastern tops. Upon turning downhill, the effort put in is rewarded by a stunning view over Auchencairn Bay to the Solway Firth. Race participants do not have the luxury of contemplating the view and need to change into downhill mode for the blast back down the route they ran up. The route downhill is fast and very technical, so care is needed, particularly when descending over the tree roots.

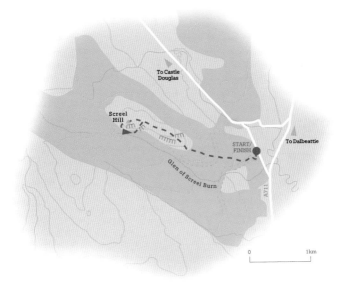

Carnethy 5 Hill Race

Distance 9km Ascent 750m Category AM Records 46:56 – Gavin Bland (1999), 54:20 – Angela Mudge (2002) Time of year mid-February Map OS Landranger 66 Website www.carnethy.com (online pre-entry only, limit 550)

A tough and very popular race early in the hill-running calendar. Exposure to harsh weather conditions, steep climbs and sharp descents are a true test of whether the runner's winter training has paid off.

Race registration is in Penicuik's Beeslack Community High School; from here, competitors are taken by bus to the race start in a field below Scald Law, 500m northeast of Silverburn. A mad charge though puddles and reeds spreads the field out before the crush to push through the bottleneck at a wall. Contestants who don't head through the gate or

over the specially constructed temporary ramp are disqualified! Once through, runners turn southwest, drop a short distance to cross a burn, then strike uphill through low heather to Scald Law's windswept summit. Following a short descent on a path trending southwest, the route departs from the path and turns southwards towards South Black Hill. After circumnavigating the summit boulders, competitors stay on a faint sheep trod to meet back up with the path coming down from Scald Law. Now keeping with this path, runners

◀ Wintry ascent of West Kip (pic: Alan Young)

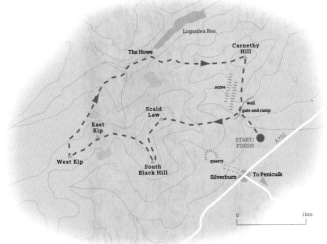

rush over East Kip, then slog up West Kip. From West Kip's summit, competitors head north, descending over grass to pick up a path down to The Howe. The route turns and climbs steeply eastwards by way of a sheltered, grassy gully. As the crest of Carnethy's western shoulder is attained, a path is picked up and shadowed onto the boulder-strewn summit. Next, runners head south through the heather on a partially marked route to avoid further erosion to the scree. After squeezing through the gate, competitors make a quick dart back to the start, where a tent awaits with hot drinks. The main prizegiving event is, however, held back at the school (where food is also available) and includes awarding a quaich to each of the runners that have completed the race 21 times.

Carnethy Hill Running Club was formed in the early 1980s for unattached hill runners looking for a club to call home. Since then, the club has evolved to become one of the largest hill-running clubs in Scotland with a diverse membership of outdoor enthusiasts. The club not only organises races across the length and breadth of Scotland, but also has a strong social side which includes weekends away, overseas trips, fun runs, video nights, parties, and lots more.

Yetholm Hill Race

Distance 12km Ascent 840m Category AM Records (clockwise) 1:02:02 –
John Brooks (2000), 1:17:03 – Clare Miller (2000) Time of year early June
Map OS Landranger 74 Website www.norhamrc.co.uk

Currently run in an anti-clockwise direction, the Yetholm Hill Race occasionally reverts to a clockwise route. Heading out is a tough slog, leaving the fast but gentle descents for the return. Part of the route follows a section of the Pennine Way, allowing runners to have one foot in Scotland and the other in England as they head back north.

The race starts from Halter Burn, 1km east of the picturesque village of Kirk Yetholm. Competitors head out southwest along a brief section of track and through a gate, then strike west directly uphill, avoiding the cattle and rushing through grass tussocks, ferns and occasional clumps of nettles. Runners risk being disqualified if they do not visit the cairn at the northeast end of Staerough Hill! Along to the trig point on the hill's main summit, the route then takes the runners down to a marshalled gap in a wall before they make a start on the slog up Sunnyside Hill. Navigation over these slopes, and Wildgoose Hill and Latchly Hill which follow, is made fairly straightforward by keeping to a fenceline. Beyond Latchly Hill's summit, the route leaves the fence and turns southwards, with runners descending over bracken to reach a sheepfold south of the burn below. Another fenceline (not marked on

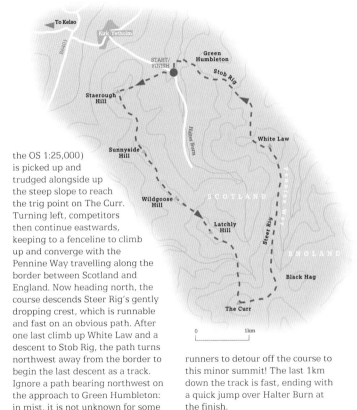

the OS 1:25,000)
is picked up and
trudged alongside up
the steep slope to reach
the trig point on The Curr.
Turning left, competitors
then continue eastwards,
keeping to a fenceline to climb
up and converge with the
Pennine Way travelling along the
border between Scotland and
England. Now heading north, the
course descends Steer Rig's gently
dropping crest, which is runnable
and fast on an obvious path. After
one last climb up White Law and a
descent to Stob Rig, the path turns
northwest away from the border to
begin the last descent as a track.
Ignore a path bearing northwest on
the approach to Green Humbleton:
in mist, it is not unknown for some

runners to detour off the course to
this minor summit! The last 1km
down the track is fast, ending with
a quick jump over Halter Burn at
the finish.

The Yetholm Hill Race raises funds for the Border Search and Rescue Unit which helps
out at the event every year. Unlike other countries in Europe, Britain's mountain rescue
teams are run by volunteers and rely heavily on donations and fundraising to provide
their invaluable free-of-charge service. So next time you are in an outdoor shop and see
a collection tin for a mountain rescue team, drop some coins in!

◀ Running the route anti-clockwise (pic: Pat Stephens)

Culter circuit

Distance **17km** Ascent **955m** Time **allow 2h45** Map **OS Landranger 72**

Easy running on a high-level route, using a fenceline for navigation and taking in fine views.

South of Biggar lie the Culter Hills – a vast range of gently rolling domes above farming, forestry and reservoirs. Culter Fell is the highest and, along with Gathersnow Hill, is designated a Graham (mountain over 2000ft). From Biggar, head south on the A702 to Coulter, then take the unclassified road south for 3km to a junction by Culter Allers Farm, where there is limited roadside parking. On foot, continue south, then veer left up the private road. Follow this road past forestry and sheep pens, then take the rough track rising uphill behind some more forestry. A few metres up this track, look for a faint path aiming directly uphill, initially over grass, then through the heather. The path becomes more obvious and passes a few shooting hides as it ascends, taking you up Fell Shin, then over more damp ground to reach Culter Fell's summit. The summit has a trig point and fine views, particularly over to Tinto and the Pentlands.

A fenceline crossing the peak from north to south can now be followed for most of the remaining route. From Culter Fell, shadow the fence

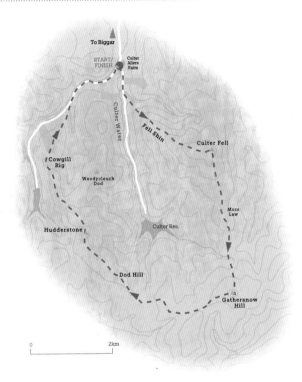

south down fine, runnable if slightly wet ground to Holm Nick where, ignoring the track, cross the burn and head directly up to Gathersnow Hill. The fence leads westwards to a small heathery nick, where you leave it to aim west by a faint trod, losing height. The fence is met again, and in mist is a real help for navigating

the next part of the route over Dod Hill and up Hudderstone. Cross the fence to the west side and start descending Hudderstone on a path. This joins a track, which takes you over Cowgill Rig, past some forestry (ideal shelter in wind and rain) and down to the road to jog back to the junction.

◀ Woodycleuch Dod

23

Durisdeer Hill Race

Distance 14km Ascent 1250m Category AM Records 1:21:53 – Rob Jebb (2008), 1:34:43 – Angela Mudge (2008) Time of year mid-June Map OS Landranger 78 Website www.carnethy.com

Some steep climbing, mainly over grass, heather and blaeberry, is interspersed with electric fencelines, occasional tracks and road crossings on this low-key event. The interesting topography adds to the adventure.

The race starts in a field just outside the small hamlet of Durisdeer and drops a short distance to cross Kirk Burn. On a faint track, the route then climbs uphill towards Black Hill, bypassing a minor hummock using a faint path on its western side. From Black Hill's summit trig point, runners bear north for a bit, then drop down very steep and rough ground to the road just north of Road-End art studio. After crossing the road and heading up a track to Dalveen Farm, competitors enter a wood. Through the first double gate, the route turns right, then slightly further on, right again onto a less discernible track to incline up through ferns and thistles and out of the wood. Upon reaching the top of the rise ahead, runners drop down to Glen Valentine, where they follow the Enterkin Burn northeast for 1km to a confluence of

waters. The route turns east and rises to a narrow col on pleasant grass-covered terrain. Over a gate is a section of steep heather-clad ground alongside a waterfall; runners descend to the burn to run to Upper Dalveen. A grassy track is climbed to reach the A702 and, after crossing the road, a direct line is made southeast by Layern Burn. The ground can be a bit tussocky before steepening for a pleasant trudge to gain 150m in height and the summit of Well Hill. Keeping to the north side of a fenceline, runners drop southwest to the next col, then begin a last ascent back up Black Hill on a vague track. A fast descent returns the runners from Black Hill's summit to the field, but you need to leave a bit of energy for the last few metres of uphill prior to the finish.

Durisdeer Parish Church seems excessively large for such a small hamlet, but it was, in fact, once the parish kirk for the Dukes of Queensberry estate. The church contains a session house and retiring rooms for the Duke of Queensberry and a remarkable mausoleum, the Queensberry Aisle, making the accessible part of the interior appear small in comparison to its external scale.

◀ The last contour before descending to the finish (pic: Hilary Spenceley)

The Merrick and Shalloch on Minnoch

Distance 18.5km **Ascent** 1300m **Time** allow 3h15 **Map** OS Landranger 77

An excellent path up the Merrick is just the start of a superb hill-running route which heads north along crests, around lochans and over several summits. A bike or additional car is needed to avoid a long return on foot.

Just beyond the car park at the end of the public road in Glen Trool, a sign points the way towards the Merrick. A fine, well-constructed path rises through the bracken to join the Buchan Burn just above the waterfalls. Shadowing the burn for a bit, the route dives in and out of forestry and down to the windowless bothy of Culsharg. To the left of the bothy, a path climbs to meet a track, which it follows to the right over a bridge, then at a sign swings north into more forest. Out of the trees, the maintained path continues to a height of 600m where it converges with a dyke. At this point, a worn path takes over, turning northeast alongside the wall. After reaching the cairn on Benyellary, the route keeps to the crest evocatively named Neive of the Spit, then makes a beeline for the Merrick's summit. Being the highest hill in the Southern Uplands, the views from the Merrick's summit are superb and vast. There are no paths leaving the Merrick's cairn and trig point to the

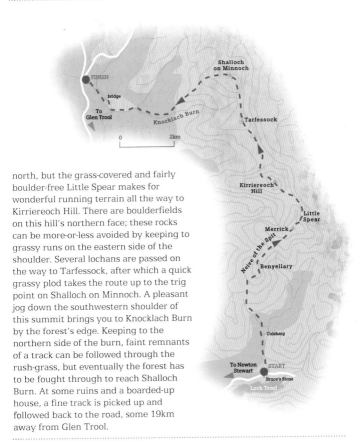

north, but the grass-covered and fairly boulder-free Little Spear makes for wonderful running terrain all the way to Kirriereoch Hill. There are boulderfields on this hill's northern face; these rocks can be more-or-less avoided by keeping to grassy runs on the eastern side of the shoulder. Several lochans are passed on the way to Tarfessock, after which a quick grassy plod takes the route up to the trig point on Shalloch on Minnoch. A pleasant jog down the southwestern shoulder of this summit brings you to Knocklach Burn by the forest's edge. Keeping to the northern side of the burn, faint remnants of a track can be followed through the rush-grass, but eventually the forest has to be fought through to reach Shalloch Burn. At some ruins and a boarded-up house, a fine track is picked up and followed back to the road, some 19km away from Glen Trool.

The Merrick Hill Race takes place in September, starting and finishing at the car park at the end of the public road in Glen Trool. The route was changed in 2008 to make the race longer but more runnable. However, this proved extremely unpopular and the race was changed back to the original loop.

◀ Looking over Mullwharchar to Corserine from the Merrick

Pentland Skyline Hill Race

Distance 26km Ascent 1850m Category AL Records 2:22:40 – Andy Kitchin (1994), 2:42:29 – Angela Mudge (2002) Time of year mid-October Map OS Landranger 66 Website www.carnethy.com

South of Edinburgh, the rolling Pentland Hills provide hill runners with a variety of training routes. The Pentland Skyline Hill Race gathers the more popular Pentland summits into a circular traverse, with the first half on obvious paths and the second half on more demanding terrain.

The route starts on a grassy path from the Midlothian Ski Centre at Hillend and heads directly for the summit of Caerketton. The trail beyond this is more worn and keeps aside a fence to the trig point and gate on Allermuir. Runners can head south down either side of the fence

Caerketton Downhill is Scotland's only downhill race, open to all. After heading to the minor summit of Hillend, the mad runners hurl themselves downhill, dropping 320m over a distance of 1.8km to Lothianburn below. The record set by Ian Wellock in 2008 stands at only 5:11 minutes!

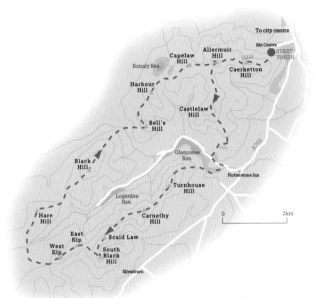

to reach a track at a col below. Following this track southwards, the course continues up to Castlelaw, then descends a steep, heather-clad hillside to rejoin the track for a fast run down to Castlelaw Farm. Participants are directed around the farm and down to dart along a short road section by Flotterstone. Through two gates, a stiff 300m climb on a path to Turnhouse is

followed by a swift descent southwest to a col. Keeping to the path, competitors continue over Carnethy to another col, then up Scald Law. Departing from the main ridge, the race turns south over grass and damp peat to take in South Black Hill, then switches back northwest on a faint sheep trod to rejoin the main trail towards East Kip. After running over the Kips, the racers drop to a drinks station on the top of the Drove Road, then enjoy a

◀ Heading up West Kip with East Kip, Scald Law and Carnethy beyond (pic: Alan Young)

Two Breweries start at Traquair House ▶

fairly flat and agreeable 1.5km run. Indicated by a post, the route leaves the Drove Road and heads onto rougher ground. An indistinct path can be taken up the gradual rise to Hare Hill's summit with its multiple cairns. Shortly after, contestants bound over burnt heather, cross wet moss and drop though dying ferns to a sharp col. After wading though water and soft rush at the col, a path alongside a wall is picked up and accompanied briefly before making a direct line on a faint path through heather to Black Hill's summit. At the summit, a boggy path is followed northeast along the crest for 1km. The path then appears to bear slightly to the left, aiming for some grouse-butts: keeping to this path is easier and, therefore, as quick as the more direct route to the col below Bell's Hill. An initial plod though ferns and reeds is left behind for a pleasant grassy climb to the summit of Bell's Hill, which can be tricky to find in mist. Now on much easier terrain, the route descends northwards on a faint path to a col, goes through a gate and shadows the fenceline over Harbour Hill. The path crosses yet another col and continues over Capelaw Hill, before dropping to a dyke with a stile. Runners slog up Allermuir, then only have to retrace their steps along Caerketton for a fast, steep descent to the finish line.

Two Breweries Hill Race

Distance **29km** Ascent **1700m** Category **AL** Records **2:33:57 – John Taylor (1992), 2:53:56 – Angela Mudge (2000)** Time of year **late September** Maps **OS Landranger 72 and 73** Website **www.twobreweries.org.uk (pre-entry only)**

This long race with rough, demanding climbs and fast track and road sections has long been regarded as a classic. A brewery at each end ensures tired competitors are rewarded with plenty of ale refreshment at the finish.

Runners collect at Broughton, where they are bussed to race registration in Traquair House grounds. The race route starts from this grand building, reputed to be the oldest inhabited castle in Scotland, and heads along the magnificent tree-lined drive onto the road. After just over 1km of road running, runners are directed into a field and onto a rough track. The track gives way to rough, open hillside where runners use a faint path cutting through grass and then heather higher up to meet the edge of the forest. A more runnable path follows the forest boundary to a nick before Birks Hill, where competitors

◄ On Black Hill (pic: Anne Nimmo)

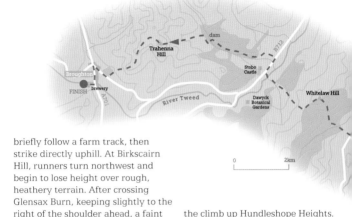

briefly follow a farm track, then strike directly uphill. At Birkscairn Hill, runners turn northwest and begin to lose height over rough, heathery terrain. After crossing Glensax Burn, keeping slightly to the right of the shoulder ahead, a faint path can be seen which avoids the tiring heather and tussocks on the climb up Hundleshope Heights. Southwest next and a faint trod can be followed to meet up with a path

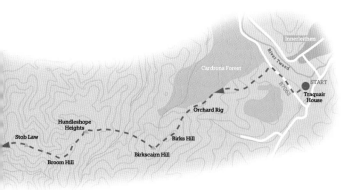

contouring north around Broom Hill's summit to the start of a sharp slog up Stob Law. Another fast and testing descent takes the route down to Glenrath Farm, where a drinks station and short section of road await. Directed onto a grassy track, runners negotiate a couple of gates and dive into forest. The track comes to a sharp corner, where the route is flagged through some undergrowth to a firebreak with a loose path ascending Whitelaw Hill. Once on this hill's crest, the course bears southwest along an indistinct path, initially through more trees, then open hillside by a wall and the forest edge. Upon reaching a col, runners go through a gap in the wall and turn northwest downhill on track that improves as height is lost. Past some buildings, the River Tweed is crossed and a quick blast along some tarmac takes contestants to a drinks station with a marshal indicating the turn to Stobo Home Farm. A very pleasant run through forest is followed by a drop to a bridge over Weston Burn to pick up a track. Beyond the bridge, the terrain heading directly for Trahenna is coarse and demanding, whereas staying on the track until it turns sharply back on itself will lead to a vague path that can be followed through the wet rush-grass. Either way, a slog up Trahenna's steep hillside awaits, by which time most runners will be starting to tire. From this last summit, a faint trod heads around Muir Burn's corrie, then keeping to the hill's crest, the route descends to a field and onto tarmac. All that is left is a run along the flat road to Broughton Ales brewery, where plenty of beer awaits.

◀ Leaping the stile on the last climb up Trahenna Hill

From the flowing Ochils and Campsies above the Central Belt to the romantic hills of Perthshire and Stirlingshire and the craggy peaks in Argyll, some of the finest hill running can be found over the many accessible peaks and mountain ranges in the Southern Highlands. Overlooking Glasgow, the Whangie and Cort-ma Law, with their crags and grass-covered slopes, are ideal for short blasts on mid-week races. To the west of Strathyre, little Ben Sheann gives an incredibly tough but short up-and-down race, contrasting with the popular Stuc a'Chroin Hill Race to the east of the village with its many long climbs. Taking to the wide tourist path on a gentle gradient, the race on Ben Lomond makes for a great spectator event, whereas on the opposite side of Loch Lomond, the classic race up the Arrochar Alps spreads runners out over several peaks and fairly pathless, grass-covered terrain. The rolling hills of the Ochils cover an area of 40km from east to west, and present a wide range of hill-running route possibilities from various villages and towns. West and East Lomond in Fife are distinctive landmarks from the south and north, and not only give good hill running but also some superb views over farmland and settlements towards the Cairngorms and Grampians. The chapter concludes with two multi-Munro-bagging days – on the long, grassy ridges of the Lawers range above Loch Tay and the circuit of peaks above Bridge of Orchy.

Southern Highlands

1 Whangie Whizz Hill Race   36
This popular race north of Glasgow is the opening event in the 'Bog and Burn' series of short hill races held mid-week throughout Central and Southern Scotland **(250m/7km)**

2 Ben Sheann Hill Race   38
A short, steep blast through forestry by Strathyre. The midges feast as runners with bare legs and arms gather at the start **(475m/5km)**

3 Cort-ma Law Hill Race   40
Big climbs, plenty of bog and rough Campsies terrain make this one of the more challenging of the 'Bog and Burn' races **(500m/10km)**

4 Ben Lomond Hill Race   42
Up and down the tourist path on one of Scotland's most climbed hills, the gradient is gentle enough to allow running all the way **(970m/12km)**

5 Lomonds of Fife Hill Race   44
A well-marked race with long trail runs on fine tracks, interspersed with steep climbs, and a fast and furious bum slide to finish **(1075m/17km)**

6 Stuc a'Chroin Hill Race   46
Often chosen as a Scottish and British Championship counter, this classic hill race becomes challenging with several steep climbs and descents **(1500m/22km)**

7 Ochil 2000s Race   48
Visiting all the 2000ft-plus summits in the Ochils, this race over rolling, grassy hills demands fine navigation skills **(1450m/29km)**

8 The Lawers Range   51
Following fenceposts and good paths, seven Munros can be bagged in under four hours **(1750m/19km)**

9 Arrochar Alps Hill Race   54
Four Munros combined in one route to make a long and demanding hill race. Much of the race route higher up is on pathless terrain, which can be tricky to navigate in mist **(2500m/24km)**

10 Above Bridge of Orchy   57
A long circular route taking in five Munros, all of contrasting character and each with different views **(2560m/28km)**

Whangie Whizz Hill Race

Distance 7km **Ascent** 250m **Category** BS **Records** 26:32 – Kamal Sanhaji (2003), 30:44 – Angela Mudge (2007) **Time of year** late April **Map** OS Landranger 64 **Website** www.westerlandsccc.co.uk

In the opening event of the 'Bog and Burn' series of short hill races, the popular Whangie Whizz gets off to a steep start, then runners test their form over a course which is never much more than a cross-country run.

The Whangie Whizz race takes place at Queen's View on the A809 Drymen Road, 7km north of Milngavie. Car parking has become an issue due to the increasing popularity of the race; therefore, runners are asked to leave cars by Auchengillan Outdoor Centre off the A809, where they are taken by bus to the start. The race begins with a blast up a steep grassy bank, sorting the runners into position. Onto a path, competitors file around a stile, then continue along the path as it twists between the rocks below the Whangie. The race then settles into a cross-country run over grass and wet

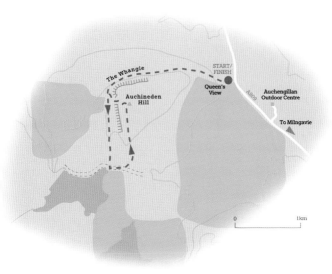

bog as it turns and aims south for a forest at the eastern end of Burncrooks Reservoir. On the approach to the forest, a track is joined and runners are sent briefly eastwards before being directed off the track and onto a faint path heading north, initially through more bog. The bog is quickly left behind on the gentle, grassy incline up to the trig point on Auchineden Hill. The route is then flagged westwards and runners descend to the Whangie path to return the same way for a fast finish on the final, steep descent.

Since 1977, Glasgow has been served by Westerlands CCC. With its large membership, Westerlands is responsible for organising some of Scotland's most popular and challenging hill races, including Ben Lomond and the Arrochar Alps. Members of the club have achieved a number of hill-running records including Manny Gorman running all 219 Corbetts in under 70 days and Charlie Campbell doing a complete round of Munros in under 50 days. In true Glasgow style, the club has a monthly social evening – in a curry restaurant!

Ben Sheann Hill Race

Distance 5km Ascent 475m Category AS Records 22:54 – Andy Kitchin (1991), 27:37 – Angela Mudge (2007) Time of year mid-June Map OS Landranger 57 Website www.stucachroin5000.org.uk

Infamous for its midges, the Ben Sheann Hill Race has an incredibly steep climb through thick forest to the summit. The return via the fast descent is such fun!

The race starts by Strathyre Primary School on the west side of the River Balvag. As runners gather, dreaded midges attack in clouds, sending even the hardiest folk away in search of a breeze. The race begins with a quick blast north alongside the road, then turns onto the marked path heading directly uphill through the forest. The route climbs fairly steeply at first, then meets a forestry track. Runners are directed north for a brief respite from climbing. A marshal points the way into some dense forest on a narrow, worn path with tree roots, rocks and branches catching out the unwary. Converging with another path, competitors are directed uphill again on a steep,

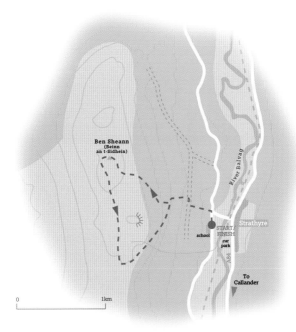

vague path. This clambers up over more demanding terrain and gradually exits the forest, fizzling out into the undergrowth on the way. Runners then haul themselves up over the thick heather to reach the summit crest, where a short dart leads them to a marshal who indicates the way down. A path twists and turns downhill, arriving at a short, flat stretch of boggy ground. Once crossed, runners continue on a

narrow path that gradually turns back northwards, crossing a burn as they re-enter the forest. The descent becomes very fast, but extreme care is needed as a trip on the tree roots or slippy rocks could have serious results. Zigzagging through the tunnel created by the trees is great fun, though, and competitors return to the road for a last quick dash to the finish.

◀ Approaching Ben Sheann's summit with Stuc a'Chroin behind

Cort-ma Law Hill Race

Distance 10km Ascent 500m Category AM Records 48:16 – John Stevenson (1999)/Kenny Richmond (2008), 53:17 – Angela Mudge (2007) Time of year early June Map OS Landranger 64 Website www.westerlandscccc.co.uk

With two major climbs on paths over grass and bog, this is one of the longer races in the 'Bog and Burn' mid-week race series, and competitors need to carry full body cover, map, compass and whistle.

Above Lennoxtown, the B822 climbs up beneath Cort-ma Law's crags to a parking area on a sharp bend overlooking Campsie Glen. The race starts on the opposite side of the road. Competitors blast off, heading east up a steep, wide grassy slope. As the slope narrows, a path rapidly forms, twisting into gaps between rocks lower down, then

rising 150m before gradually levelling out. Over undulating moorland, runners gain the first flat top and cross a fence via a stile. A few patches of wet, mossy ground are crossed as the route makes a direct line for Cort-ma Law. Around the trig point, runners then bear northwards on a faint trod over fairly flat ground, again wet in places. After arriving at Lecket Hill, a marshal directs contestants to a fence, which they follow south through soft rush, deer-grass and a few thistles to the burn below. The burn is crossed and a steep climb alongside the fence takes runners through more rush and grass to return to the stile used earlier. Runners face disqualification if they cross the fence prior to the stile! Once over the stile, runners return the way they came up with a fast, final descent to the finish line.

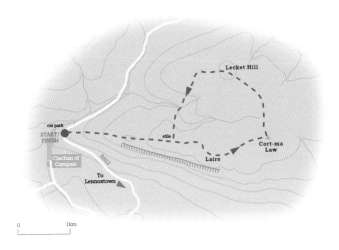

Ben Lomond Hill Race

Distance 12km Ascent 970m Category AM Records 1:05:59 – Jethro Lennox (2006), 1:16:12 – Angela Mudge (2006) Time of year early May Map OS Landranger 56 Website www.westerlandsccc.co.uk (pre-entry only, limit 175)

A race to bag Scotland's most southerly Munro, using the classic and very runnable tourist path to the top.

The race route starts from the entrance to the Rowardennan Hotel and heads north along a short tarred section of the West Highland Way to the toilets and visitor centre. It then turns sharply east and climbs up the main tourist path through the recently felled forest to enter National Trust for Scotland (NTS) land. A short, tough, zigzagging ascent takes runners to a gate, beyond which the route is marked off onto grass. The race rejoins the main tourist trail on Sron Aonaich, where there's a gentle incline to reach the bottom of the constructed zigzag path; here, the runners are again marked off left from the main path to instead climb grass and boulders, returning to the path for the last 200m or so to the summit

◀ Runners on the way up the Ben Lomond track (pic: Anne Nimmo)

trig point, where a marshal will (hopefully) offer them water and/or jellybabies. On the descent, the runners are kept on the main path all the way to the gate below Sron Aonaich, thereafter being directed slightly east off the path for 700m or so to pick up the main path just before entering Forestry Commission land. The path is followed back to the visitor centre, where a sprint is then endured back along the road to the finish.

Originally managed by the SYHA, the Ben Lomond Hill Race is one of the oldest in Scotland. From 1978 onwards, Dumbarton Amateur Athletics took on the organisation and women were allowed to compete for the first time. Westerlands CCC took charge of the race in 1995, and work with the NTS to reduce erosion concerns, hence the entry limit and the marked sections off-path. After the race, it is customary to take a dip in Loch Lomond to rinse off muck, clean up wounds and calm burning thighs. The race entry fee includes a bowl of hearty soup in a sociable atmosphere at the hotel.

Lomonds of Fife Hill Race

Distance 17km Ascent 1075m Category AM Records 1:29:22 – Andy Symonds (2007), 1:44:37 – Elke Schmidt (2007) Time of year mid-August
Maps OS Landranger 58 and 59 Website www.lomondhillrunners.co.uk

This well-marked race gives a combination of steep climbs and long trail runs on good tracks. Competitors need to plan what to wear for the bum slide down the last hill.

Registration is in Strathmiglo Village Hall, where runners make their way west along a road for 3km to a gate by a mast. The race starts from a field at the end of a track heading south from this gate. Competitors sprint up a gentle incline over grass and a few thistles to pick up a path inclining up a steep grassy gully between crags on the northern slopes of West Lomond. Higher up, the ground briefly levels, then runners climb steeply once more to the hill's summit. After running around the cairn, competitors return down the gully, then, on one of various sheep trods, run eastwards through heather to a rocky landslip and the forest beyond. Over a fence, a track is followed for 2.5km through the forest to where runners are directed onto a path switching back uphill. The climb steepens briefly, with runners clambering up loose ground and

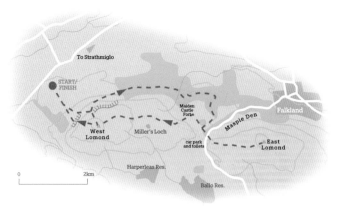

clinging onto heather, to reach a monument. Behind the monument, a track bears south, but unfortunately it doesn't last as runners are quickly directed southwards onto a vague path along a firebreak to the edge of the forest. Now on more open hillside, grassy terrain leads up to the track between the Lomonds, and contestants turn left (east) to go through a gate and down to the road. A grassy green trod through heather takes the runners onto the main track towards East Lomond, where a 1km run eastwards arrives at a gate. Through the gate and onto an uphill path, the foot of East Lomond is gained and now a stiff climb is required to attain the summit. Around the cairn, runners return to the road and back up the track to the point where it was accessed. Leaving

the track, the route crosses fine grassy ground on a fast run to Maiden Castle. From this ancient fort, some runners prefer to take the shortest line back onto the track, others bear westwards over grass and heather. Either way brings them to the track to West Lomond, where fairly flat ground leads to the foot of the hill. Back up West Lomond, tiring competitors are directed west on a vague track to cross a fence. Below is an incredibly steep descent. Runners can stay upright by gingerly making their way down, but the braver and better prepared find it much quicker to slide on their backsides to the bottom. The latter requires nerve and lycra to prevent thistles and heather from ending up in shorts! A quick sprint awaits for the short distance back to the finish.

◀ Returning to Craigmead from East Lomond

Stuc a'Chroin Hill Race

Distance 22km Ascent 1500m Category AL Records 1:59:22 – Ian Holmes (1997), 2:18:04 – Angela Mudge (2003) Time of year first Saturday in May Map OS Landranger 57 Website www.stucachroin5000.org.uk

A popular hill race taking place early in the season and often chosen as a Scottish and British Championship counter. After a straightforward run on forestry tracks, the Stuc a'Chroin Hill Race becomes challenging with several steep climbs and descents.

The well-marked route starts from the forestry cabin at the south end of the village of Strathyre. Runners go up a track climbing fairly steeply into forestry. The track makes a couple of turns, then levels out as it bears southeast, becoming gradually more grassy. Some 3km into the race, the track comes to an abrupt end, where runners are shown a faint, rough and steep path climbing directly uphill. The ground flattens out, and occasional damp sections are bounded over as the route keeps to a line of fenceposts passing

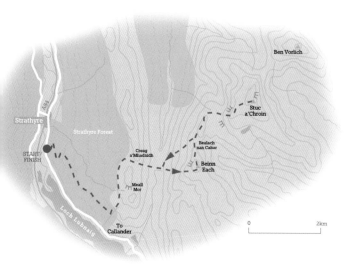

around Meall Mor. As runners approach Creag a'Mhadaidh, they are directed eastwards over a col and steep, heather-clad descent to the watershed in Glen Ample. A faint, rough path through heather follows a line of fenceposts uphill to reach more open ground and Beinn Each's summit. The route turns northwards and the race continues on an obvious well-worn path along the undulating crest. Bealach nan Cabar is crossed and a minor summit ascended, beyond which runners drop to Bealach Glas. The race continues up the grassy slope ahead to Stuc a'Chroin's summit. Competitors retrace their steps to Bealach nan Cabar, where they are directed westwards down a flagged route through heather. As height is lost, the terrain becomes more grassy and the watershed is reached. The route is retraced to the start, with tiring runners generally feeling the climbs are tougher and the track far longer than on the outward leg.

◀ Crossing the col between Creag a'Mhadaidh and Meall Mor (pic: Alan Young)

Ochil 2000s Race

Distance 29km Ascent 1450m Category AL Records 2:47:44 – Colin Donnelly (2008), 2:51:33 – Angela Mudge (2008) Time of year late August Map OS Landranger 58 Website www.ochilhillrunners.org.uk (pre-entry only)

Starting at Glen Devon, this race to climb all of the 2000ft-plus Ochils summits, with gentle climbs and descents, requires keen navigation skills as only the first and last sections are marked.

Registration is at Stirling University's Gannochy Sports Centre, where runners are then taken to the Forestry Commission's visitor car park in Glen Devon.

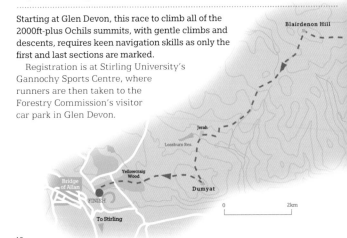

◀ Descending to Jerah with Dumyat beyond

Midge-repellent is a must for bare legs while waiting for the race to commence. The route heads initially southwest up a track into forest. As the track approaches Glensherup Reservoir, the route turns east around Black Hill and climbs out of the trees onto the northeastern shoulder of Innerdownie. Runners cross a large deer fence using a designated stile, then follow the fence southwest. Running from here onwards is on pleasant grass, following obvious fenceposts for most of the way over Innerdownie, Bentie Knowe and Whitewisp Hill to Tarmangie Hill. From Tarmangie,

returning a short distance along the path, competitors drop to the bealach below Andrew Gannel Hill and cross a fence. A path through grass is picked up and followed to the summit of Andrew Gannel Hill. Following another fence WSW,

runners enjoy a gentle drop to just under 600m, where they then leave the fence and make a beeline for The Law. Having about-turned, runners head north by the fence and obvious path to Ben Cleuch, the highest hill in the Ochils. The fence continues to Ben Buck, the halfway point at which navigation begins to get a little testing. Runners need to aim due

the route follows the fence for another 300m, then heads southwest, dropping to the confluence of the burns below. Runners turn south for a direct climb to the broad shoulder of King's Seat Hill, where a path can be followed to the summit. After

south on a faint path and pick up the source of Benever Burn. Heading for the col between Ben Ever and Ben Cleuch, they cross a fence and climb the obvious track to Ben Ever's summit. After returning to the col, the route contours on sheep tracks to the flat ground east of Blairdenon Hill. Over heather and peatbogs, navigation is tricky in mist as there are virtually no discernible features to guide. Gradually, the ground underfoot eases and a path appears which is followed to Blairdenon's summit. A fenceline crossing the summit is followed south for 600m to the point where it turns west. Runners should leave the fence here and head directly southwest for 2km over grassy ground to gradually drop down to Third Inchna Burn. The burn is crossed and a faint path picked up through the thistles. On reaching the farm at Jerah, the route sticks briefly to the track, then aims directly for the forest below, where there is a shortcut to the track to Dumyat. Higher up, this becomes faint and grassy, eventually narrowing to a path as it nears the summit. The route then follows the main tourist path towards Yellowcraig Wood. Into the trees and on vague paths through rhododendrons and over burns, runners eventually reach the eastern end of the university campus. A wall is followed for a bit until a hole is found, which runners head through to race on tarmac for the last 500m to the finish at the western end of the loch in the university grounds.

From Stirling University to Dumyat's summit and back, a mid-week race is held which follows the 'tourist-path' section of the Ochil 2000s Race described on these pages. Originally held as a competition between the university's staff and students, this race has now become very popular, attracting a field of around 300 hill runners, including some of Scotland's finest. Marked most of the way, this is a scenic hill race, but there's no time to stop as the record stands at under 33 minutes!

Ben Lawers from Beinn Ghlas ▶

The Lawers Range

Distance 19km Ascent 1750m Time allow 3h45 Map OS Landranger 51

Following fenceposts and fine paths, seven munros can be bagged in under four hours. This linear route finishes at the Ben Lawers Hotel, 15km from the start, so two cars are ideally required. However, parking is free at the hotel, provided you spend some money in the bar at the end of your hill run.

On the A827 above Loch Tay and 6km northeast of Killin, a narrow road heads northwest towards Glen Lyon. The road climbs to the northern end of Lochan na Lairige, where a cairn marks the start of a recently-built path heading northeast from the roadside. Follow this path to around 600m, where an indistinct and boggy path can be traced down to a small hydro dam. Cross the burn below the dam and pick up a boggy path heading towards another burn which tumbles down from Coire Gorm. After crossing this burn, climb directly up steep grassy ground to the small cairn on Meall a'Choire Leith's summit with its fine views across the remaining Lawers Range. Head south from the cairn to pick up a path down to the next bealach, then up the grassy slopes of Meall Corranaich. On reaching the eastern source of the Allt Gleann Da-Eig, a fainter path is taken up to the crest of Meall Corranaich's northern shoulder

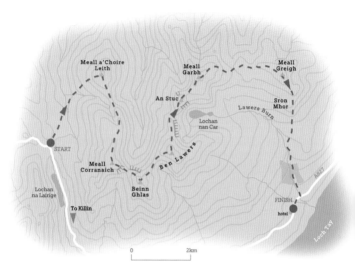

and eventually onto the Munro's summit. Leave Meall Corranaich and run east on an indistinct path which accompanies some fenceposts. The

path becomes more obvious as it twists and turns, dropping to a boggy bealach below. After crossing a worn path, climb the grassy slopes where a

Meall Garbh, An Stuc, Ben Lawers, Beinn Ghlas and Meall Corranaich from Meall a'Choire Leith

faint path gradually forms which can be taken to the summit of Beinn Ghlas. The route from here is obvious – just run down the worn path, then climb the steps on the constructed path to the busy trig point and large cairn on Ben Lawers' small summit, with its excellent views in all directions. On a vague path giving a fine, runnable descent, head north from Ben Lawers and lose nearly 200m of height. A slight rise is reached and bypassed on the left (west) following a faint path. Drop another 100m on a fairly obvious path to a bealach, then run up a path to the grassy summit of An Stuc. Upon reaching the end of An Stuc's grassy crest, a sharp rocky drop blocks progress – look for a path heading slightly to the east. A bit of easy scrambling on rock and loose grass is encountered as you quickly descend to the next col. On grass and between rocks, an obvious path climbs out of the col to Meall Garbh's summit, which is reached in a matter of minutes. Meall Greigh sits some distance from the group's main cluster of Munro peaks; however, it is linked by a line of fenceposts from Meall Garbh, alongside which a path runs down to a boggy bealach. To the east, the path continues up to Meall Greigh's summit, passing an unusual erratic boulder on the way. From this last Munro, drop ESE on a faint path, then south down Sron Mhor to cross wet heathery ground and pick up an obvious worn path which joins the fence marking the NTS boundary. Follow a path down to farm buildings and pick up a track to reach the road by the Horn Carver, where food and a pint can be had at the nearby Ben Lawers Hotel.

For many years, Ben Lawers was thought to be over 4000ft. However, towards the end of the 19th century, the Ordnance Survey measured it at 3983ft. A cairn was, therefore, built in 1878 to take the mountain above the magic height, but unknown to the group of men who constructed it, summits are measured to the base of the cairn, so the height remained the same. The cairn has long since disappeared and only a small cairn and trig point now sit on the top.

Arrochar Alps Hill Race

Distance 24km Ascent 2500m Category AL Records 3:07:39 – Billy Bland (1987), 4:09:26 – Christine Menhennet (1987) Time of year late June
Map OS Landranger 56 Website www.racentries.com (limit 150)

Situated to the west of Loch Lomond, the Arrochar Alps consist of several high peaks, four of which are Munros that combine to make a demanding long hill race. Considering how popular this mountainous group is, it comes as a bit of a surprise to find how much of the race route higher up is on pathless terrain, which can be tricky to navigate in mist.

Registration is in the new community hall in Arrochar, and the race begins on the track heading to Succoth Farm. There are several checkpoints on the route, but runners are free to find their own way between them. As the race begins, runners are directed onto a path through Glen Loin. At the end of the

glen, the path heads into some forestry and drops to a bridge over Inveruglas Water. Runners then head up to a hydro road above the river and follow it for 1km towards Sloy Dam. A small cairn at the side of the road marks the start of a steep, winding path that runners can choose to slog up to the crest on Ben Vorlich's southern shoulder. Alternatively, runners can opt to continue running up the road to the dam, then turn northeast for a very steep climb up to the crest. Both routes lead to an obvious path on the crest wandering to Ben Vorlich's summit cairn 150m north of the trig point. Competitors return southeast for a punishing run down a 500m

◀ Heading up Ben Vane from Sloy Dam (pic: Ian Nimmo)

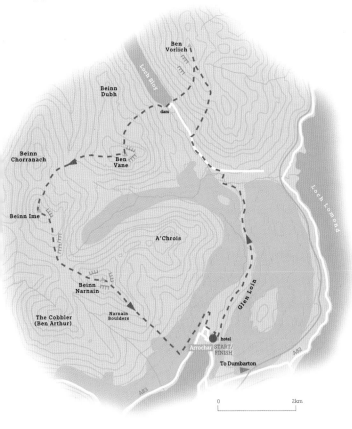

steep drop to Sloy Dam. After crossing the dam, the route follows the road up until it switches back on itself, then crosses boggy ground to

start climbing steep grassy slopes. There are no paths to assist runners, they just climb southwest until gradually the ground levels out

55

higher up. Ben Vane's summit can be seen ahead with a green grassy bank cutting through the rocks to the crest above. It's a quick run from the top of this bank to the small summit cairn. Aiming west on pathless grassy slopes, runners descend quickly from Ben Vane to the col below. After crossing one burn, competitors climb upstream by the burn tumbling down from Beinn Ime. This burn is crossed higher up; then, before Glas Bhealach is reached, the route turns south and inclines uphill over heather, avoiding a few crags, to pick up a path as it approaches Beinn Ime's summit. Leaving the summit behind, runners descend by a worn path travelling southeast along the crest. The path begins to turn southwards and lose height over increasingly boggy and grass-covered terrain. After traversing a boggy bealach with its fence, a path is taken – initially through soft rush and grass, then boulders higher up – to reach Beinn Narnain's summit cairn and trig point resting on a flat bouldery plateau. Below is the last descent of the race, where runners head southeast on a worn path twisting through the crags and rock. Further down, heather and ferns are bounded over as the route takes the line of the old cable railway to the forestry track below. Turning left, runners follow a marked route back to the finish. The prizegiving takes place back at the hall, where a small memento is given to the few runners who manage to complete the course in under four hours and everyone partakes of the food and real ale courtesy of race sponsors Fyne Ales.

Above Bridge of Orchy

Distance 28km Ascent 2560m Time allow 6h30 Map OS Landranger 50

Starting from Bridge of Orchy Station, this long circular route takes in five Munros, all with contrasting characters and each with very different but equally stunning views.

From the large car park by the Bridge of Orchy Hotel, go over the road to the railway station up the hill. Using the underpass, cross to the other side of the station and up to the West Highland Way. Take the path ahead that turns left in front of a phone mast. This path enters Coire an Dothaidh, ploughing through some incredibly mucky and boggy sections in the process. Higher up, the soggy ground is left behind and you reach a cairn on the pass

between Beinn an Dothaidh and Beinn Dorain. Turn SSW for a 1.5km uphill run on a path to a large well-built cairn. This is on Beinn Dorain's northern top and in mist might be mistaken for the summit! The mountain's true summit is a brief jog southwards into and out of a dip, and affords stunning views in all directions. Return to the large cairn on Beinn Dorain's northern top, then on a wide and pathless grassy ridge run eastwards towards Meall Garbh. A short section of scree is followed by an excellent downhill run, bearing northeast over grassy ground to meet the Allt Coire a'Ghabhalach at around 500m. After

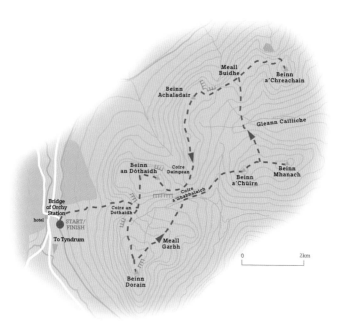

Meall
Buidhe

Beinn
a'Chreachain

Beinn
Achaladair

Gleann Cailliche

Beinn
an Dòthaidh

Coire
Daingean

Beinn
Mhanach

Beinn
a'Chùirn

Coire
a'Ghabhalaich

Bridge
of Orchy
Station

Coire an
Dothaidh

hotel

START/
FINISH

To Tyndrum

Meall
Garbh

0   2km

Beinn
Dorain

crossing a burn, contour around the grassy hillside below Coire a'Ghabhalaich to pick up the track below Beinn a'Chuirn. Follow this track up to a burn, then climb directly up the steep, loose, grassy slopes of Beinn a'Chuirn. On a faint path, run down to the gate on the bealach between Beinn a'Chuirn and Beinn Mhanach, then aim directly east over easy ground to the Munro summit. Return to the gate, then aim northwest, bounding downhill over

grassy ground to pick up a burn that leads you to the Allt Cailliche below. After crossing this river and a couple of tributaries further on, aim up the grass-covered ground over Garbh Mheall to reach Meall Buidhe. Pick up an obvious path heading northeast to the col below Beinn a'Chreachain, then slog up scree and bouldery ground to the summit crest, where Beinn a'Chreachain's cairn lies a brief distance uphill to the south. Taking care, run back down the scree and boulders to the col, then return on the path to Meall Buidhe. Continue southwest along the path over runnable ground to the boggy bealach below Beinn Achaladair with its tired fence. A steep path zigzags up the hillside ahead and reaches Beinn Achaladair's long summit crest. After passing the cairns on the tops, run along the path which gradually turns south to drop to a grassy col, then climb up to a small cairn on Beinn Achaladair's south top. Fine downhill running is next, following the path to the pass above Coire Daingean and Coire a'Ghabhalaich. The path becomes briefly indistinct approaching the col, then more obvious as it crosses the bealach and inclines uphill over grassy ground to the south top of Beinn an Dothaidh. The main summit cairn is a short jog further on. From Beinn an Dothaidh's summit cairn, run over to the western top and take in some final views for the day. Turn south and drop to a path which is followed to the bealach between Beinn an Dothaidh and Beinn Dorain, then return to Bridge of Orchy via the outward route.

Inverness

6
2 Newtonmore

Dalwhinnie
3
1 8
Fort William
5
10 7
4
9

The **Central Highlands** stretch from the Great Glen to the A9. Contained within this wonderful mountainous area, the higher, rougher mountains of Lochaber with their steep climbs and long ridges contrast with the vast plateaus above sculpted corries further east. Originating from Highland Games, the Meall an t-Suidhe and Creag Dhubh Hill Races do not reach their respective hill's main summits, but instead attain only minor summits, enabling spectators to watch runners over the entire routes. With no descents, simply a short climb on forest tracks and mountain biking trails, the Aonach Mor Uphill Race is gentle on the knees. Though fairly short, the route up Beinn a'Chuallaich gives fine off-path hill running, rewarding the little effort taken with stunning views. Brutal, technical descents on loose rock, slippy grass banks and a downhill path ensure the Ben Nevis Hill Race is not for the faint-hearted. The Monadh Liath can be a bleak place to test navigation skills, but the terrain is a joy to run over. Ossian and Alder Forest are beautiful and remote areas, requiring a bit of planning to access but well worth the effort. Fabulous high-level ridge running is enjoyed whilst Munro-bagging above the Black Mount and along the Mamores range.

Central Highlands

Meall an t-Suidhe Hill Race

Distance 4km Ascent 465m Category AS Records 27:48 – Gavin Bland (1999), 33:44 – Angela Mudge (1999) Time of year early July Map OS Landranger 41 Website www.lochaberac.co.uk

Also known as the Melantee Hill Race, this tough little blast doesn't actually reach Meall an t-Suidhe's summit, but instead heads to the top of a crag on the hill's northern shoulder. The race used to be part of Lochaber Highland Games, thus the route was chosen to allow most of the race to be viewed from the playing fields below.

As with the Ben Nevis Hill Race (p70), the Meall an t-Suidhe Hill Race starts with a blast around the racetrack at Claggan Park in Fort William to spread the competitors out. Runners then head out of the park onto the road, and are almost immediately directed over a verge onto a hidden track skirting around the back of the playing fields. Swinging east, the track continues for 500m before fading into the undergrowth. In the past, this next section would involve bounding over grass, reeds and wet bog; however, there is now a faint but discernible path to follow. After a gentle climb, this path crosses a small burn (not marked on OS maps) and dives into

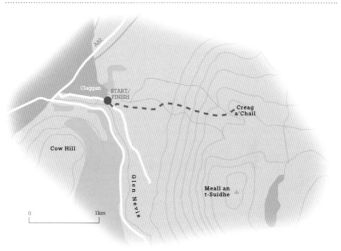

thick ferns. An incredibly steep ascent now begins, quickly gaining 250m in height. Leaving the ferns behind, the path zigzags uphill to another burn, where the gradient starts to ease. The race 'top' on the summit of Creag a'Chail, is reached and runners about-turn, taking care not to charge into other runners still heading uphill. If conditions underfoot are wet, runners 'in the know' will have prepared for the slippy descent by wearing lycra shorts to aid bum-sliding down part of the route! Back down on flatter ground, the return along the track feels longer than on the way in, but on entering the playing fields, competitors are cheered around the track to the finish.

The Meall an t-Suidhe Hill Race is now part of a weekend race series called the Triple Hirple. Organised by Lochaber Athletic Club, the series comprises three races, with Meall an t-Suidhe being the first to take place on Saturday afternoon. Next up is the Half Ben Nevis Race on Sunday, which follows the Ben Nevis race route as far as the burn crossing at around 670m, then returns via the infamous Green Wall. The third race is Cow Hill Race on Monday evening, which takes competitors along Fort William's High Street up to the mast on the hill's summit and back. All are excellent training for the Ben Nevis Hill Race later in the year, and a prize mug is awarded to all runners that complete the three races.

◄ Running around the track to Melantee's finish

63

Creag Dhubh Hill Race

Distance 6km Ascent 380m Category AS Records 27:07 – Jon Brooks (1997),
32:21 – Angela Mudge (2006) Time of year first Saturday in August
Map OS Landranger 35 Website www.newtonmorehighlandgames.co.uk

As part of Newtonmore's Highland
Games, the Creag Dhubh Hill Race is a
short run through a lovely birchwood
to a minor summit on this hill's northeastern shoulder.

Highland Games hill races tend to
start and finish with a dart around
the games field and often send
runners only as far as spectators can
see. Being part of the Newtonmore
Highland Games, the Creag Dhubh
Hill Race is no exception. Great for
spectators, the atmosphere at the
start builds up the competitors'

adrenalin. Once out of the northern
end of The Eilan (where the Games
are held), the route crosses thistly
fields, then passes through a gate to
meet the River Calder. Having
enjoyed a good soaking trying to
wade through the river, runners
climb up an embankment and cross
the A86 to start running up a farm
track. The track enters a birch forest,
where the contestants are pointed
onto a path which rapidly becomes a
narrow trod through heather. This
section of the race can be

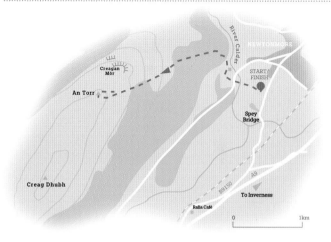

frustratingly difficult to overtake on. As the route leaves the trees, contestants clamber over rocky sections using the heather to haul themselves up. Overtaking becomes easier further on where the heather becomes more stunted. The gradient steepens and the minor summit of An Torr (meaning 'Lower Hill') with its large cairn is reached. After passing the cairn and summit marshal, competitors head straight back down the way they came up, or stick briefly to a trod slightly to the left of the path and rejoin the path lower down, thereby avoiding the runners still climbing uphill. Back through the river and across the fields, runners return to the games where spectators cheer as they make a final lap around the track to the finish. In past years, runners' efforts were rewarded by a medal, but now with the sponsorship of Dalwhinnie Distillery, each competitor is given a miniature of a 15-year-old malt.

Centuries ago, Scottish clans lived without much peace. When oncoming trouble was sensed, a Crann Tara (or Fiery Cross) would be lit to summon people to battle. It became an honour to run with the cross ablaze, and men competed for the privilege. Highland Games were, therefore, born, with the first recorded Games being the Braemar Gathering of 1064. Fortunately, clans are no longer war-like, but the popularity of Highland Games persists – with the hill run being central to the event. Women can now take part too!

Aonach Mor Uphill Race

Distance 4km Ascent 600m Category AS Records 22:15 – Robbie Simpson (2009)
26:28 – Nicola Meekin (2009) Time of year New Year's Day Map OS Landranger 4:
Website www.lochaberac.co.uk

A short blast up Aonach Mor's northern slopes on forest tracks and mountain bike trails to the Snowgoose Restaurant is the perfect cure for a Hogmanay hangover. A fine spectator event from the restaurant or gondola.

The race takes place in the Nevis Range car park, 6km northeast of Fort William and is well marked for most of its route. From the southwest end of the car park, a marked track is followed uphill into the forest. The track twists and turns as it makes its way up a steep section, followed by a forest trail on a gentle incline. The trail switches east on a flat, grassy track, giving a brief respite from the climb; then continuing through the forest, the route changes direction and starts to aim directly uphill along the line of the downhill mountain-bike trail.

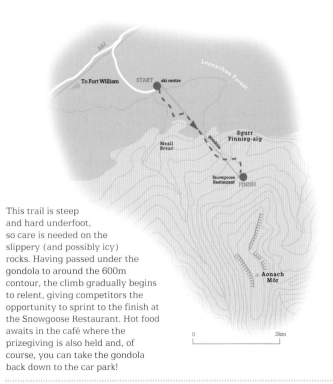

This trail is steep and hard underfoot, so care is needed on the slippery (and possibly icy) rocks. Having passed under the gondola to around the 600m contour, the climb gradually begins to relent, giving competitors the opportunity to sprint to the finish at the Snowgoose Restaurant. Hot food awaits in the café where the prizegiving is also held and, of course, you can take the gondola back down to the car park!

There are only three regular uphill races in the Scottish hill-running calendar. Aonach Mor Uphill takes place on New Year's Day, and again in late July, and Glas Tulaichean Uphill is run in early June. The Aonach Mor Uphill held in July is organised by Off Beat Bikes and, not surprisingly, the records are slightly faster than those set on New Year's Day. On the Continent, many of the hill races are uphill only as, unlike in Scotland, there's a good chance of finishing in warm sunshine and chilling out at the top in a café or mountain hut.

◀ Approaching the Snowgoose Restaurant on the Aonach Mor Uphill Race (pic: N. Price/teamcruachan.co.uk)   67

Beinn a'Chuallaich

Distance 6.5km Ascent 600m Time allow 1h15 Map OS Landranger 42

Beinn a'Chuallaich is a quiet hill reached by bounding over grass and heather-clad slopes. A huge cairn rests on the summit where superb views can be enjoyed in all directions.

Beinn a'Chuallaich lies directly above the small village of Kinloch Rannoch, which can be accessed using narrow roads from Loch Tay to the south, Pitlochry to the east or the A9 to the north. To the east of Kinloch Rannoch, the B847 climbs towards Trinafour. On this road, by the northern edge of a spruce forest, there are some sheep pens with an area to park. On the other side of the road a large gate in a high deer fence denotes the start of the hill route. Go through the gate, cross a field and drop to a small white corrugated bothy. Step over the little burn behind the bothy, then strike

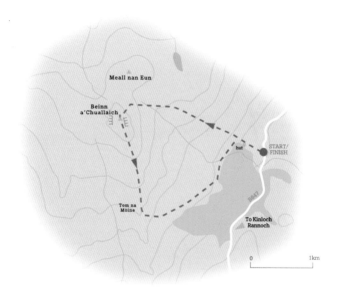

directly uphill through thick ferns. The ferns give way to heather and the gradient eases. Now on more runnable terrain, Beinn a'Chuallaich's eastern slopes come into view. Aim for the bealach between Beinn a'Chuallaich and Meall nan Eun and, upon reaching it, turn south and climb directly to the Corbett's summit. A trig point and large cairn rest on the crest, with a magnificent 360-degree view that can be savoured on clear days. Turn SSE to start running down a faint path with Schiehallion dominating the view ahead. Height is lost fairly quickly as feet run over grass and between occasional boulders. At around the 600m contour and on more level ground, turn southeastwards and aim for a wall that can be seen at the top of the forest below. Hugging the western side of the wall, a vague path can be picked up to wind your way through the heather. Sticking to this trod makes for fast progress back to the white bothy and the roadside.

◀ Beinn a'Chuallaich from the southeast

Ben Nevis Hill Race

Distance **14km** Ascent **1350m** Category **AM** Records **1:25:34 – Kenny Stuart (1984), 1:43:25 – Pauline Haworth (1984)** Time of year **first Saturday in September** Map OS Landranger 41 Website www.bennevisrace.co.uk (pre-entry only and limited to 600)

The oldest and most popular race in the calendar, this is a great spectator event. The descent is renowned for being rocky, fast and unforgiving!

After piping the competitors around the Claggan Park games field, the Ben Nevis race starts with a blast around the track at the park. Runners then charge onto the road, heading southeast. Over a distance of 1.5km, the field is spread out, then at the Nevis Inn at Achintee, the tourist path is picked up and the uphill racing begins. Some runners prefer to follow the path with its

occasional switchbacks all the way. However, there are a couple of shortcuts that some runners take, though these involve climbing over slippery grass and deep bracken with no overtaking opportunities. Further on, the path turns northeast and the gradient steepens. At a sharp corner, competitors leave the path and turn east, climbing up loose, wet rock and briefly over grass-covered terrain to rejoin the main path just before Red Burn. Here, runners briefly rehydrate from the cool, clear water. The path is left almost as soon as it is

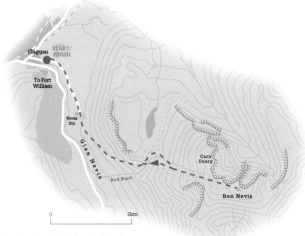

joined and contestants head directly uphill on a grassy slope. The grass doesn't last and before long runners are clambering up rock and scree, trying to make a direct line for the summit. The main path is rejoined once more for the last 250m of ascent to the summit. Upon reaching the summit, runners hand over a token, then return initially the way they came up. Upon reaching the path just before the Red Burn crossing, runners have the option of aiming west, directly down the Green Bank to the tourist path below. This route travels down very steep, loose and wet grass-covered ground with boulders hiding amongst the tussocks – not for the faint-hearted! Back on the tourist path, contestants retrace their steps towards Claggan. With wobbling legs from the descent, a tiring last mile run back along the road from Achintee has to be endured. However, upon entering the games field, competitors are spurred on to the finish by cheering spectators.

First held in 1899, the Ben Nevis Hill Race is the oldest hill race in Scotland. Although injuries on the race tend to be minor, there has been one fatality, where in blizzard conditions a runner died of exposure after losing a shoe. The Ben Nevis Hill Race is, therefore, not to be underestimated and all runners must carry full kit, including waterproof body cover, map, compass, whistle and food.

◄ Heading up the tourist path (pic: Keith Jeffrey)

Monadh Liath

Distance **23km** Ascent **1050m** Time **allow 4 hours** Map **OS Landranger 35**

Gentle slopes combine with faint paths aside old fenceposts for delightful running over vast moorland and glacier-carved landscapes.

From Newtonmore's main street, Glen Road heads up the side of a café through the town's outskirts towards Glen Banchor. At the end of the road, there is a parking area below a moraine. To the right of the moraine a northbound track skirts the edge of a forest. Leaving the forest behind, the track continues up a glen where, 1km further on, a small cairn marks a hidden path leading down to the Allt a'Chaorainn. Amongst birch, a wooden bridge crosses the river to the western bank, where a faint path takes you north, then turns to aim for an old hut tucked into the hillside. Some of the inscriptions

scribbled on the hut's internal wood are more than 100 years old. The path can subsequently be followed across the hillside beyond. The peak of A'Chailleach, with the path scarred up the heather on the hill's southern rise, dominates the view ahead. A large cairn rests on the hill's summit, with plenty of room to shelter out of wind. Descending north from A'Chailleach's crest on a vague path, height is quickly lost. The ground abruptly drops to a small burn, which is easily crossed. Ahead, run across wet ground with occasional peatbog to reach a line of fenceposts travelling west to east. Turn east by the posts for a few minutes to reach Carn Sgulain's two small, untidy cairns. About-turn and enjoy easy running as you accompany

◀ The old hut above the Allt a'Chaorainn

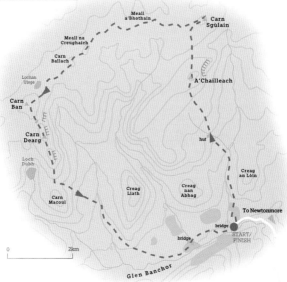

the fenceposts westwards towards Carn Ban for 5km. Closing in on this minor top, the terrain changes from a pleasant grass-covered plateau to a boulder-strewn landscape that requires a bit of concentration. Having ascended Carn Ban and reached the cairn, swing south and leave behind the fenceposts that have so far made navigation a doddle. Drop to a bealach with a small narrow lochan, then climb up to the small cairn perched precariously on Carn Dearg's summit. Some fine ridge running is enjoyed, traversing the southern top down to a col ahead of Carn Macoul. From the col, steep ground is easily descended into Gleann Ballach, where you bound through heather to cross to the eastern bank of the Allt Ballach. Now aiming southeast over grassy terrain, occasional deer and sheep trods can be picked up to ease progress through the heather. As the ground levels out, the unoccupied house and buildings at Glenballoch come into view. Leaping over bog and grass tussocks, aim directly for the buildings, then pick up a fine track to return to the car park at the road end.

Ossian Munros

Distance **26km** Ascent **1550m** Time **allow 6 hours** Maps **OS Landranger 41 and 42**

A rail journey over moorland into a remote and beautiful area with Loch Ossian at its heart. An enjoyable day's hill running is topped off with hearty food at Corrour Station House while waiting for the return train.

In the wild interior of the Grampian Mountains, Loch Ossian sits alone surrounded by forests and hills. Access is by one of several long hiking or biking routes; however, the train to Corrour Halt is not only faster, it is also a wonderful way to enjoy the changing views of this remote area. If Corrour Station House is open when you arrive, make a reservation for food later in the

day. Cross the railway line and follow a track east towards Loch Ossian. The track splits prior to reaching the loch. Turn left and, just after the track turns sharply east, look for a boggy path heading northwards. Obvious at first, the path eventually fades into the hillside, though the terrain thereafter is undemanding and fairly runnable. Beinn na Lap's western shoulder is reached and a faint path is followed to a small ruin, north of which is a lochan and the summit cairn. Return to the ruin, then descend southwards through grass and thick heather towards the western edge of the forest which lies

◀ Beinn na Lap above Corrour Lodge

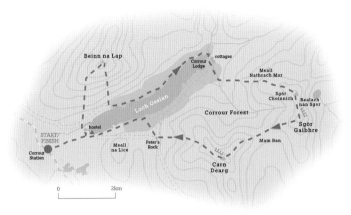

directly below. A pleasant run leads along the track to Loch Ossian's eastern end. Built in 2003 using Spanish granite, Corrour Lodge is situated by the water's edge and has a dramatic glass frontage looking back down the loch. Jog around the lodge, cross the bridge over the River Ossian, then, at a junction in the track, keep left and pass some cottages, outbuildings and a warehouse. The track becomes rougher and continues uphill to a small dam. Cross the dam and aim directly for Meall Nathrach Mor. Heather gradually gives way to more gentle terrain, making for swift progress to Sgor Choinnich's summit. After bearing south to Bealach nan Sgor, twist uphill on a faint path to the small cairn on Sgor Gaibhre's summit. Leave the cairn and turn WSW to jog down a path to Mam Ban Bealach, passing a few large erratic boulders on the way. The path continues up to Carn Dearg's summit with fine views westwards. Head down Carn Dearg's northwest shoulder for 1km, then drop westwards to Peter's Rock. This small memorial stands by a junction on the old drove road. From here, head northwards to reach the edge of a forest, where an obvious firebreak takes you directly down to the track. Turn left for a pleasant jog along the shore and past the SYH eco-hostel (booking advised if looking to stay) to return to the station, where food hopefully awaits.

Alder Forest

Distance 24km (+30km on bike) **Ascent** 2000m (+500m on bike)
Time allow 6h (+1h30 on bike) **Map** OS Landranger 41

In the heart of remote Alder Forest, Culra Bothy is surrounded by high mountains with vast plateaux and long ridges giving excellent running, mainly on paths and over grass. Good navigation skills are essential!

Park by the rail crossing just down the road from Dalwhinnie Station and bike down the track on the western shore of Loch Ericht for 8km to a junction just before Alder Lodge. Turn right and head uphill to the highest point on the track, then descend past a shed to reach Loch Pattack, where the track follows the shore to a wire and wooden bridge. Cross this, negotiate some peatbog, and wheel along the track towards Culra Bothy. Just before the bothy, there is a footbridge back over the

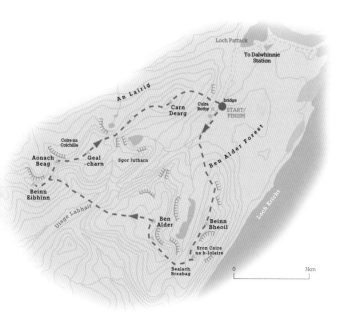

Allt a'Chaoil-reidhe: leave bikes here and cross the bridge. Now on an excellent path initially following the river's south bank, turn right (west) and run for 2.5km to a point where the path takes a sharp turn southwest. Leave the path here and cross heather and grass with occasional hidden boulders to head up Beinn Bheoil's northern shoulder.

On the gravelly surface that covers the crest, you'll find a small cairn denoting Beinn Bheoil's summit. Leave the cairn on a vague path to bear southwest over the bouldery plateau of Sron Coire na h-Iolaire, and pick up a faint path crossing Bealach Breabag. The path zigzags a boggy route up through the rocks to reach Sron Bealach Beithe: the ridge

◄ Carn Dearg from Loch Pattack

beyond takes you northwest to Ben Alder's vast plateau with the highest lochan in Britain. The summit trig point, cairn and superb views lie a few minutes to the northeast. From Ben Alder's summit, easy running over grass takes you WNW for 2km. Running down wet, heather-clad slopes, the Uisge Labhair is reached and crossed. Head directly uphill over heather, then grass to reach the ENE shoulder of Beinn Eibhinn. Pick up a well-defined path, turn left and follow the edge of the coire to the summit. Return along the ridge, then continue northeast on the path to the bealach before Aonach Beag: the summit is reached by a quick, sharp uphill pull. On Aonach Beag's summit, head east on pathless ground for a bit. The path reappears approaching the next bealach and is followed uphill to Geal-charn's small summit cairn resting above Coire na Coichille with some cracking views. On Geal-charn's vast pathless plateau, head northeast to the edge of Coire Cheap. Turn right (east) and with some careful navigation, find the ridge that heads northeast between the two coires. A fine path travels down to the narrow bealach, then continues over the wide grass-covered bump of Diollaid a'Chairn. One last grassy climb leads to a boulderfield and Carn Dearg's summit. Leave the summit by a path heading northeast. The descent steepens, then, as it levels out, turn southeast and drop down grass, heather and wet ground to Culra Bothy and your bike.

Above the Black Mount

Distance **32km** Ascent **2100m** Time **allow 6h45** Maps **OS Landranger 41 and 50**

Old paths and tracks aid access to high peaks that look down deep corries to the vast lochan-pitted landscape that is the Black Mount.

From the Bridge of Orchy Hotel, a narrow road heads around the western shores of Loch Tulla to Victoria Bridge, where there is a large car park. The road splits into three beyond the bridge: take the left fork past a house and farm buildings. After 1.5km, the fine track reaches a green bothy, which used to be the old schoolhouse, behind which you'll find a stalkers' track travelling north. Follow this for 2km to cross a burn, then climb directly

uphill on a path twisting through the heather. Higher up, the path disappears into boulders. Stob a'Choire Odhair's summit, with its fine outlook over the Black Mount, is reached shortly thereafter. Heading WSW, a path gradually forms and is followed down to the bealach. Cross the bealach, and continue uphill on the path as it turns southwest through loose scree and eventually reaches the grassy east end of the Aonach Eagach. Turn west and follow a faint path to a notched ridge with some entertaining but easy scrambling. The ridge is left behind and a bealach is met with a

79

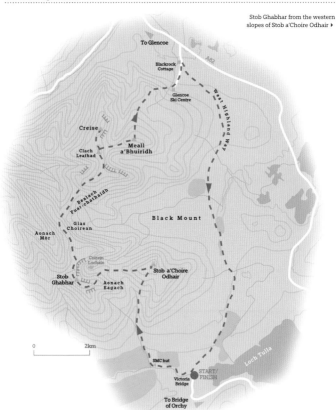

Stob Ghabhar from the western
slopes of Stob a'Choire Odhair ▶

To Glencoe

Blackrock
Cottage

A82

Glencoe
Ski Centre

West Highland Way

Creise

Meall
a'Bhuiridh

Clach
Leathad

Bealach
Fuar-chathaidh

Glas
Choirean

Black Mount

Aonach
Mòr

Coirein
Lochain

Stob
Ghabhar

Aonach
Eagach

Stob a'Choire
Odhair

0   2km

SMC hut

Loch Tulla

START/
FINISH

Victoria
Bridge

To Bridge
of Orchy

thick iron post marking the start of
a fenceline leading up to Stob
Ghabhar's summit cairn. Leave the
cairn and run northwards down
pathless terrain to a wide, grassy
crest. Although height is gradually

lost over the next kilometre, there
are a few minor rises with
occasional boggy patches to cross,
before the bealach above Glas
Choirean is reached. Climb one
more rise, then turn northeast and

80

drop over fairly pathless ground to grassy Bealach Fuar-chathaidh. Aim northeast up steep, grass-covered hillside to loose, stony ground higher up. This levels out and becomes enjoyably runnable to reach Clach Leathad's summit. Pick up a path and aim generally northwards through boulderfields. Upon reaching a wide plateau, keep an eye out for a cairn on your right marking the later route to Meall a'Bhuiridh. Before taking this, gain Creise by a path over more gravel, boulders and grass. Then return to the cairn noticed earlier, aim east and scramble down a couple of awkward moves. Jog down a path to a bealach, then continue up over stones and scree to arrive at the Meall a'Bhuiridh summit cairn with a superb view to Rannoch Moor. Keeping west on the slightly higher ground above the ski tows, descend Meall a'Bhuiridh's grass-covered northern shoulder. Having dropped to the hut at the base of the ski tow, a track can then be followed to the top of the main chairlift. A worn path meanders downhill through the heather and under the chairlift to the main Glencoe Mountain ski centre and café. A fine run awaits along an 11km section of the West Highland Way from Blackrock Cottage to Victoria Bridge.

The Mamores

Distance **31km** Ascent **3475m**
Time **allow 8h30** Map **OS Landranger 41**

One of the finest mountain ranges in
Britain, the Mamores has ten Munros
linked in a long chain, giving
excellent high-level ridge running.

Just west of the Polldubh Falls
in Glen Nevis, and opposite the
old cottages at Achriabhach, a
track leads south into forestry.
Immediately left of this track,
a path climbs directly uphill
through the dense forest,
crossing a forestry track
further on to reach another

Glen Nevis
To Fort William
Polldubh Falls
START/FINISH
Achriabhach
Mullach nan Coirean
Stob Ban
0   1km

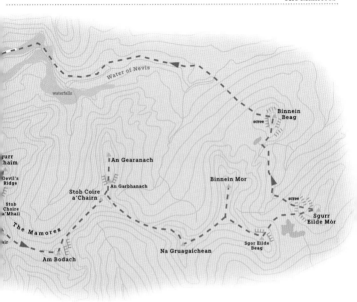

track higher up. On this track, aim south for a short distance until a small cairn on the right is found: this marks the start of an old, steep and now very overgrown path twisting and turning uphill through the birch forest. Above the trees, heather is clambered over to reach the wide crest of Mullach nan Coirean's northeast shoulder. Now at a runnable incline, a path is followed to a rough and narrow ridge, where boulders and scree lead to the cairn on Mullach nan Coirean's summit. Leaving the cairn behind, on excellent runnable terrain, follow a

path southeast over a minor top, then east to bypass a rocky summit. Descend grass and boulders to a col, then slog up loose scree to Stob Ban's airy summit. Head a few paces south from the summit, then look for a path heading east through a gap in the rock and drop to grass-covered terrain below. Cross the outflow from Lochan Coire nam Miseach, then follow the old stalkers' path up to the bealach between Sgurr an Iubhair and Stob Choire a'Mhail. Now on the 'Devil's Ridge', proceed north over Stob Choire a'Mhail, then drop down a short notched gap. The path drops

◀ Binnein Mor and Ben Nevis from Sgurr Eilde Mor

83

to the left and avoids any difficulties, climbing up out the other side of the gap. After one more drop, a slog up a path zigzagging through the quartzite brings you to Sgurr a'Mhaim's summit with superb views to Ben Nevis. Return along the ridge and head up Sgurr an Iubhair, then on more runnable terrain, descend southeast and push up to Am Bodach. Scramble northeast down very steep and loose ground to cross the grassy bealach and follow the path up over a minor top to Stob Coire a'Chairn's bouldery summit. An Gearanach requires a detour from the ridge. Use a path that zigzags north through scree to reach a bealach, then climb up to the crest. Although the route is obvious, there are one or two tricky moves crossing from one side of An Garbhanach's narrow crest to the other. On reaching An Gearanach's summit, about-turn to the bealach below Stob Coire a'Chairn. Head southeast and pick up a faint trod to reach the path on the main ridge around 500m east of Stob Coire a'Chairn's summit. Cross more grass, then clamber up loose rock to attain Na Gruagaichean's northwest top. The main summit lies beyond another dip, with more loose ground to ascend. On an obvious path, aim east to cross a col and run up to Binnein Mor's south top. A detour north over grassy ground, then boulders is required to gain Binnein Mor's main summit. Return to the south top, then run down delightful grassy slopes to Sgor Eilde Beag, where a cairn perched above Coire an Lochain marks a steep, grassy descent to the northern end of the lochans. A faint path can be picked up for a direct ascent of Sgurr Eilde Mor and, although the terrain is loose and bouldery, there are no difficulties in attaining the summit. Return a few metres along the crest and look for a path heading right. A bit of scree-running will bring a smile to your face before reaching grassy ground and a steep drop to the burn below. Cross the burn, then

Although the Mamores present a real challenge to most hillwalkers and runners, the route is but a part of a longer circuit of peaks called Ramsay's Round. Starting from the Glen Nevis Youth Hostel, the task is to run along the Mamores, head east to Beinn na Lap, then return over the Loch Treig hills, the Grey Corries, the Aonachs, Carn Mor Dearg and Ben Nevis to the youth hostel. That's 23 Munros – and the record stands at 18 hours 23 minutes! If the thought of that is too exhausting then you can try Tranter's Round which misses out the Loch Treig hills and Beinn na Lap.

Stob Ban from Sgurr a'Mhaim ▶

follow a stalkers' path to the lochan at the foot of Binnein Beag. Skirt around the south end of the lochan and follow a path up through the boulders and scree to the summit. Head west down steep ground over boulders and scree, then bound through heather to reach the Water of Nevis. Cross this river to pick up the Glen Nevis path and return west to Steall with its superb view of the waterfall tumbling down from the ridge above. Further on, run down the fine path above Nevis Gorge and reach the road end, where a 3km jog downhill to Achriabhach awaits.

To the east of the A9, long glens, vast plateaux, dark corries and rocky tors have been sculpted by the glaciers of the last ice age. The barren arctic tundra on the mainly granite Cairngorm plateau is surrounded by smaller grassy and heather-covered hills in Abernethy, the East Mounth, Drumochter and Feshie. To the southeast of the Cairngorms, fine tracks over Mount Keen, Clachnaben and the hills above Loch Muick make for rapid access to peaks with superb views. To the southwest of Loch Muick, Glenshee offers excellent winter skiing and long runs over grassy plateaux. Further south, the terrain above Pitlochry and Dunkeld offers fine cross-country running through dense forest to discover hidden lochs. Ben Rinnes, Meall a'Bhuachaille and Geal Charn to the northeast of the Cairngorms give fine hill running along heather-clad crests. And the Cairngorms themselves offer endless opportunities to explore routes across the vast high-level terrain, with one challenge, in particular, taking in all of the 4000ft-plus peaks.

The Cairngorms and the North East

Mount Keen by the Mounth Road

Distance 16km Ascent 690m Time allow 2h15 Map OS Landranger 44

The Mounth Road, an old drovers' route, gives excellent trail running, approaching Mount Keen from the Dee to the north or, as described here, the Esk to the south.

Near the end of the public road at the western end of Glen Esk, there is a car park and noticeboard by a bridge over the Burn of Branny. Cross the bridge, passing the neighbouring church and turn up the next drive on the right. As this approaches the House of Mark, turn left, go through a gate and run along a grassy track. After passing some forestry, you come to a large old gate: beware of the electric fence either side! Now on a more bouldery track, continue up Glen Mark to Queen's Well, an unusual crown-shaped structure, built over a spring in honour of Queen Victoria. Ahead the holiday-rental of Glenmark is passed, before fording Easter Burn and Ladder Burn. Difficulties will be encountered when attempting to cross these burns in spate, though they should still be passable. Further on, the track climbs fairly steeply above Ladder Burn, then turns and

heads up to a cairn on flatter ground. Mount Keen can now be seen clearly ahead, with the track veering slightly to the left of the crest. At the trackside 1km further on, a large cairn sits on the heather. From here, a recently constructed path makes for fine running to near the summit. Shortly after passing a strange, almost headstone-like rock with a carved letter 'B', Mount Keen's summit trig point resting on a rocky platform is reached. Standing alone above glens, the views from the summit towards Lochnagar and the Cairngorms are stunning. Return by the same route – if you enjoy downhill running, the fast descent to Glenmark is a hoot.

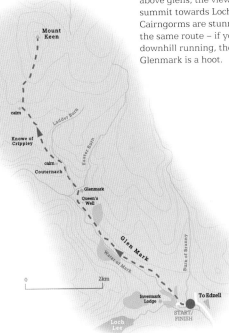

Meall a'Bhuachaille Hill Race

Distance 10km Ascent 640m Category AM Records (previous course) 50:37 –
Jethro Lennox (2006), 55:48 – Angela Mudge (2005) Time of year late October
Map OS Landranger 36 Website www.highlandhillrunners.org.uk

Forestry tracks and a thigh-busting climb up steep heather-clad slopes lead to a fine hill traverse with a superb 360° panorama of the Cairngorms, Monadh Liath and Moray.

Previously starting from Glenmore Lodge, the Meall a'Bhuachaille Hill Race now begins at the Badaguish Outdoor Centre, just north of Loch Morlich in the heart of the Cairngorms National Park. The race has more trail running and less bounding through heather than before. From the Centre, the race heads southeast on a track for 500m to a junction, from where the route turns northeast with a gentle climb. A sharp turn on the track is met, where runners then head up a faint path through moss and heather following the edge of a small area of forest. Where the trees end the path disappears abruptly into the undergrowth and runners then do battle with thigh-deep heather, sharp juniper bushes and hidden boulders on the ever steepening climb ahead. Gradually the ascent eases and the heather thins to signal the approach to Creagan Gorm's summit. After running around a tidy little cairn, competitors head south on a faint

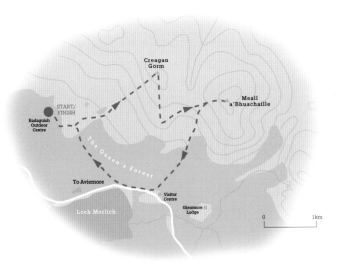

trod through heather, losing 100m of height. Upon reaching a level area, the route turns northeast and converges with the path crossing the bealach between Creagan Gorm and Meall a'Bhuachaille. On this path, a short, steep climb takes the runners to Meall a'Bhuachaille's summit cairn. Participants run around the cairn and return down the path, avoiding others still climbing. Just before reaching the bealach, the path splits and competitors descend on a well-maintained path into forest and on to Glenmore Youth Hostel. A track is then followed for 2km uphill back to the race finish at Badaguish Outdoor Centre.

A fine, runnable alternative route to the race heads up to Meall a'Bhuachaille's summit via its eastern shoulder. From the end of the road just beyond Glenmore Lodge, bear northeastwards along the Ryvoan track for just over 1km to reach An Lochan Uaine ('The Little Green Loch'). This is a peaceful spot, secluded amongst old Scots pines and below steep scree. About 1km further on is Ryvoan Bothy, where a well-maintained path heads up the eastern slopes of Meall a'Bhuachaille. On an easily runnable gradient, the path travels to the summit with its small cairn and fine views over the Cairngorms and the Monadh Liath.

◄ October snow on the Meall a'Bhuachaille Hill Race (pic: Keith Burns)

Geal Charn above the Braes of Abernethy

Distance 16km **Ascent** 600m **Time** allow 2h30 **Map** OS Landranger 36

Such enjoyable hill running! If it wasn't for the vast Cairngorm panorama seen from Geal Charn's crest, you might think you were in the Southern Uplands.

On the north side of the river in Nethy Bridge, an unclassified road heads east, over a crossroads and through the area known as Causar to arrive at a junction after 3km, where a narrow road heads southeast towards the Braes of Abernethy. At the end of this road, there is limited parking by a turning circle and an impressive new block of stables. On a fine downhill track, run through a gate and pass derelict Dorback Lodge and a couple of other houses. Bear right after some dog pens and follow the track downhill for a bit to jog briefly past a wood and over a bridge. The views abruptly open up. Continue southeast by the fine track, on a gentle incline just perfect for sustained running. After 6km, the track reaches a small green hut just beyond its highest point. Here, a path takes over, bearing southeast initially, but soon after striking westwards uphill to reach an unusual memorial with a long slate sword embedded into stone. A short distance beyond, the path disappears into tussocky wet ground and peat hags, which makes for slow progress as you ascend the gradually rising ground. On meeting a broken line of fenceposts which travels along the crest from Geal Charn Beag to Geal Charn over stunted heather ground

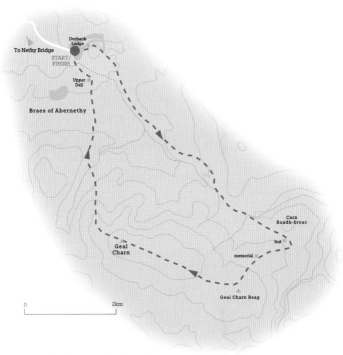

cover, running becomes both easier and more enjoyable. Superb views across to Ben Avon and the Cairngorm plateau can be savoured on clear days, while making rapid progress along this section. A small cairn marks Geal Charn's summit, where a line of fenceposts points to the northwesterly descent route. As height is lost, the fenceposts are left behind and gradually thickening

heather is bounded over while running downhill. After crossing the Allt na h-Eirghe and continuing over grassy and slightly wet ground, pick up a track that leads to the ruined cottages at Upper Dell. Once through a gate in a fence, take a sharp left turn and follow a faint track to cross Dorback Burn and return to the road end.

Clachnaben Hill Race

Distance **15km** Ascent **965m** Category **AM** Records **1:14:20 – Ian Holmes (2000),
1:25:04 – Angela Mudge (2000)** Time of year **mid-April** Map **OS Landranger 45**
Website **www.cosmics.org.uk**

Starting northeast of Clachnaben, forest tracks give the impression of a straightforward run to a popular summit. Don't let this initial impression fool you, this is a tough race with some incredibly rough running through the heather.

The normal hillwalking route is on paths and tracks, starting from Spittal Cottage to the southeast on the B974. To reach the start of the race route, however, cars full of anticipating runners are directed off the unclassified road, 6km to the north of Spittal Cottage and along a forest track. The race starts in the middle of the forest at a forest track junction (GR642902) and bears initially southwest along the track. After 2.5km of track with a few changes of direction, runners are directed across a fence and the forest is left behind. Turning sharply left, a worn path running parallel to the forest edge is followed down to cross a couple of burns. The path carries on uphill through the grass, wet in places, then levels out a bit. A sheep

trod travelling slightly west of the crest of Threestane Hill can be picked up. After entering a grassy corrie, then rising to a bealach, the route is marked to Mount Shade's summit. Heading west, an obvious path is picked up to run down to the next bealach, where a rough path travels to Clachnaben's summit tor. Having run around the tor, competitors bear southwards, picking up a faint and boggy path buried in the heather. It's difficult to say whether keeping to the path is easier than bounding over the heather: either way the terrain is rough on ankles and knees. The route gradually turns east and drops down to cross a burn. A track at the bottom of a wood is followed east for 200m to the edge of the trees, where runners are directed along a faint path which climbs quite steeply to return to Mount Shade. The route then aims directly back to the forest by Burn of Greendams, where the track is rejoined and the route retraced for 1.5km to a junction. Runners are directed east along a grassy track that eventually turns, with one last incline for a sprint to the finish line.

The race is organised by the Cosmic Hill Bashers and supported by Deeside Brewery, who provide refreshment at the finish! The Cosmic Hill Bashers are based in the Aberdeen area and not only organise training, races and social events, but also have their Cosmic Championship, the Krunce Series and Summer Series for members to compete in.

◄ Approaching Clachnaben's summit tor (pic: Alan Young)

Deuchary Canter

Distance **18km** Ascent **900m** Category **AM** Records **1:30:50 – Andy Symonds (2009), 1:38:42 – Angela Mudge (2008)** Time of year **early March** Map **OS Landranger 52** Website **www.wildoutdoors.info/running.htm**

On fine tracks and paths hiding in the forested hills above Strath Tay, this race gives fast and enjoyable trail running, possibly on snow cover.

The well-marked race starts from the back of the Dunkeld House Hotel and heads up a track to meet the old A9. Competitors run east along the road for 200m, then turn onto a track travelling around a small loch. The route climbs uphill through forest, then on a narrow, rooty path, turns and contours under Craig a Barns. If you happen to run this route outwith the race, a lovely view can be savoured from here down to Strath Tay. Back to the race a fast, sharp drop is followed by an abrupt change in direction to climb back uphill on a mucky, twisting path. The path's gradient eases, then swings northwest and converges with a flat forestry track on which runners continue north for 700m. Markers point northeast to a small rising path, which meets another forestry track, becoming quite muddy when back in the forest higher up. As the

route approaches Mill Dam, competitors are sent off-track over heather in the direction of Deuchary Hill. Fortunately, after crossing another track further on, the terrain is easier, continuing on an obvious path which cuts through the heather. As runners close in on the base of the hill, markers should show the direct clamber that the route takes to the crag on the summit. After running around the top, competitors bound down over thick heather and pick up a faint path on the northern edge of Lochan na Beinne. This is followed down to a forestry track which gradually sweeps back to the south. The route returns to Mill Dam, runs around the loch's southern shore, then follows a smooth forest track towards Dunkeld. There is one last heathery climb by a path before the final descent to the finish.

The Deuchary Canter is the third and final race in the Highland Boundary Races, which are held over a weekend in March. On Friday night is the short Tay Dash where headtorches light the route through the forest at the Hermitage. Saturday sees another fairly short race in the form of the Birnam Hill Classic. Prizes are awarded for the individual races and for the series as a whole.

◄ Running down to Mill Dam

Beinn a'Ghlo

Distance **20km** Ascent **1350m** Time **allow 3h15** Map **OS Landranger 43**

Long, wide grassy crests above scree and heather-clad slopes are accessed using one of several fine tracks aiming in from the south.

To the northeast of Blair Atholl stand the three Munros collectively known as Beinn a'Ghlo. The hills are most readily accessed from Blair Atholl by the minor road to Old Bridge of Tilt and then on towards Monzie Farm, where parking is available near the road end by a gate and cattle grid. Alongside a forest, carry on to the end of the road, pass through a gate and run along a track for 1.5km to a couple of sheds behind a fence. Cross the fence using a stile, then run over grass and boggy ground, leaping across a small burn on the way. A path travelling parallel

to an old dyke is picked up and followed. Keep to the path as it leaves the wall, then climbs directly through the heather to boulderfields higher up. As the ground begins to level out a cairn is seen ahead: unfortunately, this is not Carn Liath's summit, which is a quick jog 300m further on. From the summit, bear initially northwest on a path which loses gradual height along the wide crest. A fairly sharp drop leads to a narrow bealach, where a worn path heads up the southern shoulder of Braigh Coire Chruinn-bhalgain. The path becomes fainter higher up, but the route to the small summit cairn is obvious. Leaving the summit behind, on fairly pathless ground, navigation in mist can be tricky. Bear

◀ Carn Liath from Loch Moraig

east along the crest and descend slightly to a small grassy plateau. Continue northeast for 300m, then drop east over grass to another bealach. A path can be seen heading east through the grass to the wide col between Airgiod Bheinn and Carn nan Gabhar. Northeast of this col, an easy climb leads to a summit crest with three bouldery tops, the highest being the furthest away. Return southwest along the crest to the col, then climb up over Airgiod Bheinn's narrow rocky summit. A couple of

short scree runs can be used to aid an otherwise tricky bouldery descent to reach the Allt Bealach an Fhiodha. On the opposite side of the burn, fast running can be enjoyed on an excellent worn path through the heather. The path contours around the base of Beinn Bheag, then converges with the track to return to Monzie.

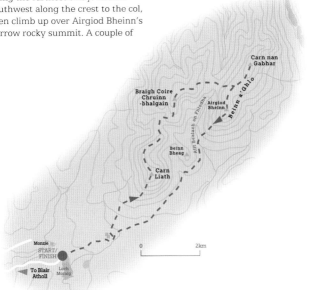

Ben Rinnes Hill Race

Distance **22km** Ascent **1550m** Category **AL** Records **1:56:55 – Andy Symonds (2009), 2:21:21 – Angela Mudge (1996)** Time of year **late July**
Map **OS Landranger 28** Website **www.dufftownhighlandgames.org**

As part of the Dufftown Highland Games, this well-marked race on tracks and paths is an excellent introduction to long hill races.

The race starts with a sprint around the games field, then exits onto Hill Street. Heading west, runners are directed south onto a track and the climbing begins. The track converges with the end of a road and turns west, dropping slightly to some new housing and trees. After a right turn slightly further on, the track continues up through a narrow, fenced channel between fields, then passes through a gate. Briefly into a wood, where the track disappears, the route follows markers around the edge of golf fairways on Dufftown Golf Course. Beyond a tee, the route crosses soft rush and deer grass to a fenced corner. Now on heather, a faint path is followed to the trig point sitting at the northern end of Little Conval's traces of ancient fort. An obvious zigzag path heads down its heather-clad southern slopes towards Glach-

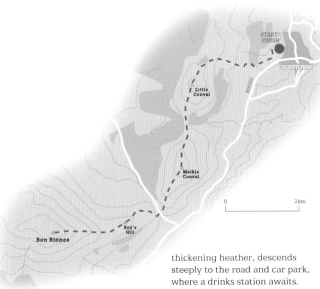

en-ronack; however, the race takes a less distinct but more direct line. From the bealach, a wet trod is followed directly up Meikle Conval. Bearing southwest, the route drops to some peat hags and, through thickening heather, descends steeply to the road and car park, where a drinks station awaits. Through a gate, runners follow the tourist route up to the summit crag of Ben Rinnes, before retracing their steps to Dufftown. Upon entering the games field, runners have to do a lap of the track, cheered on by the large crowd of spectators.

The highest summit northeast of the Cairngorms, Ben Rinnes boasts stunning views, particularly northwards over the Moray Firth to the hills of Ross and Sutherland. This makes it a popular hill, suffering from the effects of boot traffic. Recent work to curb erosion has included reconstructing the path up the steep section on Scurran of Lochterlandoch, creating a narrow zigzag with rocky steps. Being fairly technical to descend at speed, this kind of path would normally cause runners to brake; however, it didn't seem to slow down Andy Symonds in 2009, who broke the course record that had been set before the zigzags were put in place.

◀ Runners heading up the tourist route to Ben Rinnes

Above Loch Muick

Distance **26km** Ascent **1280m** Time allow **4h** Map **OS Landranger 44**

A very runnable high-level circuit on well-defined paths. Dark Lochnagar's cliffs and crags contrast with the flat grass-covered plateau that surrounds it.

From the car park at the end of the public road in Glen Muick, pass the rangers' hut, then turn right at the track junction and continue to the houses at Allt-na-giubhsaich. On a marked path, circumvent the buildings and head through forest, then up a track to its highest point where a cairn marks the path branching off towards Lochnagar. Follow this well-

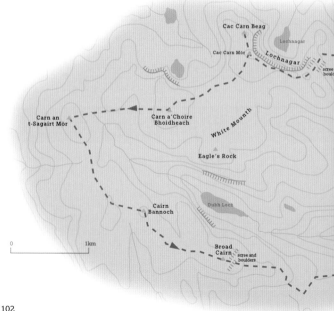

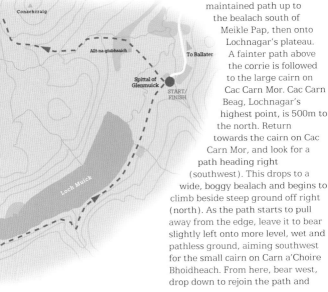

Conachcraig

Allt-na-giubhsaich

To Ballater

Spittal of Glenmuick

START/ FINISH

Loch Muick

maintained path up to the bealach south of Meikle Pap, then onto Lochnagar's plateau. A fainter path above the corrie is followed to the large cairn on Cac Carn Mor. Cac Carn Beag, Lochnagar's highest point, is 500m to the north. Return towards the cairn on Cac Carn Mor, and look for a path heading right (southwest). This drops to a wide, boggy bealach and begins to climb beside steep ground off right (north). As the path starts to pull away from the edge, leave it to bear slightly left onto more level, wet and pathless ground, aiming southwest for the small cairn on Carn a'Choire Bhoidheach. From here, bear west, drop down to rejoin the path and

▲ Cac Carn Beag from Carn a'Choire Bhoidheach

follow it southwest. Cross two burns 500m apart, then aim west over grass and climb directly to Carn an t-Sagairt Mor's summit. From this peak's southern cairn, descend southeast by an initially faint but increasingly obvious path. The ground becomes more runnable as the boulders are left behind. After crossing a wide bealach, Cairn Bannoch's bouldery summit is attained quickly. Once beyond Cairn Bannoch's boulders, a faint path heads over grassy ground to Broad Cairn with its clamber up bouldery ground to attain the summit. East from Broad Cairn's summit is more bouldery ground, which can be tiresome and tricky to cross. Leaving this behind, pick up a track and follow it down to the pony shed. Take the fine path heading directly down to Loch Muick, and enjoy a quick 5km trail jog along the southern shore to return to Spittal of Glenmuick.

Just north of Carn an t-Sagairt Mor's summit, you will encounter some scattered plane wreckage, including a large section of wing. These pieces are the remains of a Canberra jet that crashed into the hill in 1956, sadly killing all the crew. The remains of more than 50 military planes can be found on Scottish hills, including some WWII German fighters in the Pentlands, USAAF bombers on Skye and RAF planes in various locations.

Glenshee 9 Hill Race

Distance 30km Ascent 1690m Category AL Records 3:20:16 – Tom Owens
(2009), 4:13:31 – Claire Gordon (2008) Time of year early August
Map OS Landranger 43 Website www.glenshee9.co.uk

The Glenshee 9 Hill Race will test navigation skills in mist but, given a clear day, the route over grass and faint paths is wonderfully runnable.

South of Braemar, the A93 climbs to its highest point at 665m above sea level. The Glenshee Ski Centre is a few metres to the north, and this is where the Glenshee 9 Hill Race starts. Runners gather by the ski tows at the eastern end of the large car park and are set off, climbing initially through heather and tussocks as they aim southeast in the direction of Meall Odhar. The ski tracks are quickly picked up to run past huts and snow fences, meeting the top of the ski tow on Meall Odhar, beyond which the ground briefly drops to a wide col. Ahead a

Back in 2005, some running mates and myself headed out to bag the Glenshee Munros in winter conditions. We posted our route on the web and it generated interest as a possible hill race. Al Hubbard took forward the idea and in 2008 the Glenshee 9 Hill Race was born. Part of the Scottish Long Classic Series, the race now attracts around 70 runners, and generates much needed funds for the Braemar Mountain Rescue Team.

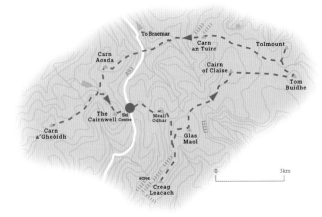

path can be seen aiming directly up Glas Maol, with another fainter path contouring to the right below the hill's crest. The route takes the gradual rise of the contouring path onto Glas Maol's southwestern shoulder, then converges with a line of wooden fenceposts. Running along the fenceline over grassy terrain to a bealach, old wire hidden in the grass can trip up unwary runners. As the ground becomes rocky and boulder-strewn, runners need to concentrate on footwork as they climb beside a wall to Creag Leacach's small, untidy summit cairn. Returning to the bealach and wooden posts, the route then follows a line of iron posts until the ground begins to level. The posts are left behind as competitors make a beeline for Glas Maol's summit trig point and cairn. Turning north, the

route drops over a gentle, grassy slope and picks up a track heading north, then northeast to cross the wide plateau towards Cairn of Claise. As the ground starts to rise, the ridge ahead tempts with a more direct line to the summit; however, the ground here is bouldery, unlike the faster, runnable terrain of the grassy track. Upon reaching the large summit cairn on Cairn of Claise, a wall heading eastwards can be followed before ending abruptly. From here, a line of fenceposts can be traced down the grass and tussock-covered ground. A path gradually forms, which takes runners over the undulating ground of Ca Whims to the small pile of stones on Tom Buidhe's summit. The route returns for a short distance towards Ca Whims before a faint path whisks runners northwest towards a burn. After crossing the water, the route continues north over peat hags and tussocks to pick up a line of fenceposts which lead to the top of Tolmount. Retracing steps for around 500m, an indistinct path now leaves the posts and aims westwards through the heather and peat hags, dropping into a dip. Bearing generally northwest, careful navigation is required over the next 2km of featureless terrain. Carn an Tuirc gradually comes into view and, as it is neared, a path can be seen crossing the col before it. This takes a grassy line to the boulderfield on Carn an Tuirc's summit. Having reached the small summit cairn, runners need to drop westwards; however, the route over the boulders is not initially obvious. One of several vague paths can be picked up to descend through the boulderfields and heather to the boggy ground below. The paths converge, crossing the Allt a'Gharbh-choire where one of two paths running parallel to the north bank of the river is taken to an old bridge. After crossing the A93, an incredibly steep and pathless ascent through deep heather on Carn Aosda's northeastern shoulder awaits. Beyond, the gradient gradually eases and the heather is left behind for a short run over

gravel to Carn Aosda's summit. A fine track leads westwards, then drops and turns to a bealach, where runners leave the track for a faint southbound path over damp ground. The col between The Cairnwell and Carn nan Sac is attained and a well-worn path is picked up to head over some minor tops. Upon reaching a lochan, a fainter path can be traced which skirts southwest around its southern shore, avoiding an ascent of Carn nan Sac. The path gives a gradual rise onto the grassy crest between Carn nan Sac and Carn a'Gheoidh, becoming more obvious as it approaches the last rise up the Munro. Having run around the summit cairn, tiring competitors return to the col between The Cairnwell and Carn nan Sac. Directly ahead a loose, worn path cuts through heather, rising to meet the main gravel track which passes the top of the ski lift on the way to The Cairnwell's summit with its array of masts and huts. One last descent is all that remains, and the quickest way to do this is to return to the top of the ski lift and charge directly downhill over grass and tussocks to the café below. Hot food and a prizegiving is held in the café, where runners have a chance to swap tales of the day's route.

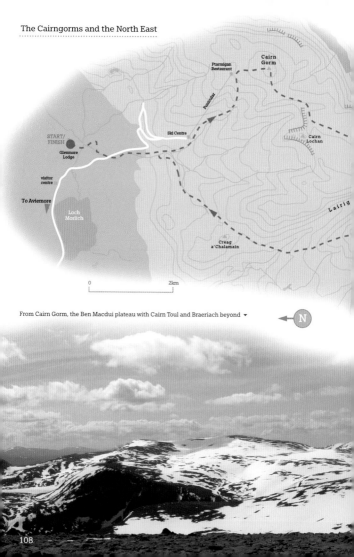

From Cairn Gorm, the Ben Macdui plateau with Cairn Toul and Braeriach beyond ▼

Cairn Gorm

Ptarmigan Restaurant

Funicular

Ski Centre

Cairn Lochan

START/FINISH

Glenmore Lodge

visitor centre

To Aviemore

Loch Morlich

Lairig

Creag a'Chalamain

0   2km

N

Cairngorm 4000ers

Distance 33.5km **Ascent** 2600m
Time allow 7h
Map OS Landranger 36
Website www.shr.uk.com

With summits sitting on wide
plateaux above deep, sculpted coires
and high cliffs, skilful navigation is
required to run across two high
mountain ranges divided by the
famous pass of the Lairig Ghru. In
winter, this route is only suitable for
those experienced in running in
winter hill conditions.

Starting from Glenmore Lodge,
2km east of Loch Morlich, this run
heads south out of the grounds
and crosses a track to reach a
bridge over the Allt na Feith Duibhe.
Once over the bridge, a track is
followed for 350m to a junction.

Turning right (west), another track takes you for 350m to a bridge over the Allt Mor. Immediately before this bridge, a sign points to Coire Cas, where a fine path with two wooden walkways is followed to the Cairngorm Mountain Ski Centre. Behind the centre, take the track which follows the route of the funicular railway to reach the bottom of the White Lady ski tow, then aim for the Ptarmigan Restaurant. From here, a well-marked path leads to Cairn Gorm's large summit cairn. Turning west, a path drops over grass and small boulders to contour around a minor summit ahead. On boulder-strewn ground, the path climbs a gentle incline to the cairn on Stob Coire an t-Sneachda. After descending west to the next col, the path swings south, then contours over the grassy slopes below Cairn Lochan to reach Lochan Buidhe. Gravel and occasional rock is climbed to gain Ben Macdui's summit trig point and viewfinder. The route, now pathless, turns southwest and drops steeply on boulders and then scree and heather to the Lairig Ghru some

700m below. Cairn Toul towers above and ahead, with rock outcrops and cliffs. These difficulties can easily be avoided by aiming to the left or right, but either way an incredibly steep trudge will be needed to gain the rocky crest 700m higher up. There are two cairns on Cairn Toul's summit, beyond which a short, bouldery descent of 150m leads to an equally brief climb up more boulders to Sgor an Lochain Uaine. Turning WSW over lichen-clad boulders, the terrain gradually eases and a path is followed above crags onto the flat plateau of Carn na

Criche. Now on very runnable ground, the burns above the Falls of Dee are reached and crossed, beyond which there's a gentle rise with more boulders. Braeriach's dramatic summit is attained, with its cairn perched above the high cliffs dropping into Coire Bhrochain. Pick up a path and follow it east, then northwards over Sron na Lairige down to the Lairig Ghru. One last climb up into the Chalamain Gap – created by meltwater being forced uphill by a glacier in the last ice age – then it's a fast run on the fine path to return to Glenmore Lodge.

The Cairngorm 4000ers is one of a number of recognised long-distance hill runs in Scotland that unofficial records are kept for. In 1963, Eric Beard recorded a time of 4:41 on this route, Mel Edwards recorded a faster time in 1980, then Dan Whitehead shortened it further in 2001. After five failed attempts, Alec Keith took it down to 4:22 in 2004. All of these records were set without running up Sgor an Lochain Uaine, which was promoted to Munro summit status in 1997. In 2007, Paul Raistrick darted over the Munros, including Sgor an Lochain Uaine, in an incredible 4:00:16! The fastest time by a woman is 6:45 and was set by Kath Butler in the 1980s. More of these long-distance hill runs can be found at www.shr.uk.com/longdistance.aspx

◄ Braeriach with Ben Macdui distant

Inverness

Fort William

To the west of the Great Glen and south of the Rivers Bran and Carron, long mountain ridges head westwards above sparsely populated glens towards the Hebrides. Although modest in height and never far from a road, the peaks in Ardgour, Moidart and Sunart are rough and fairly demanding. The Munros to the west of Loch Lochy combine to give a challenging hill race, whereas, a few miles to the southwest, a trail race along forest tracks below Druim Fada is enjoyed near the end of the year. On the outer edges of the Rough Bounds of Knoydart, several ridges and mountains can be run up, including Sgurr an Utha and Beinn Sgritheall which require little effort to attain breathtaking views. The mountains become higher and more demanding further north, and superb ridge running along the crests of the South Glen Shiel Ridge and the circuit above Mullardoch can be enjoyed on clear days. Exploring the eastern outer fringes of this area, you'll find the hills become gentler, but not any less dramatic, as the Strathconon hills and Meall Fuar-mhonaidh testify, being distinctive landmarks and a joy to run along.

West Highlands

Druim Fada Chase

Distance **10km** Ascent **430m** Category **BM** Records **0:45:00 – Ruari Watt (2008),
0:55:01 – Roxy Bannerman (2008)** Time of year **November**
Map **OS Landranger 41** Website **www.lochaberac.co.uk**

Starting with a climb through dense forest, the terrain levels off on this superb race over fairly flat ground and down gentle slopes.

After parking cars by the entrance to Annat Point Industrial Estate in Corpach (just northwest of Fort William between Loch Linnhe and Loch Eil), runners collect at race registration in the house opposite, which is where the race finishes. Groups of competitors are then ferried by bus to the race start at the bottom of the road heading up to Loch Eil Outward Bound Centre. The race begins with a sprint up the road to the centre. Past the main building and between huts, runners reach the

centre's fire assembly point, where a small lane leads to a fenceline. Competitors turn right, then on a faint path, follow the fenceline uphill into thick forest. The path becomes more distinct, with a burn below and a fence on the right to guide runners to a gate further on. Through the gate, the route crosses the burn by a wooden bridge, which can be slippery when wet. Now with the fenceline on the left, runners climb uphill through the forest, avoiding fallen trees and taking care on roots. Another gate is reached, beyond which the dense forest is left behind and a vague path is taken uphill through heather to eventually meet

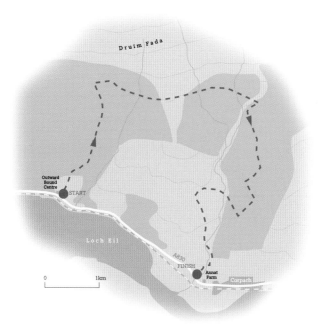

a track contouring the slopes below Druim Fada. The track is followed eastwards for 3km, then as it starts to drop gently, another track is met and runners turn right, aiming southwest, then southwards downhill. Keeping to this track for 2km, losing gradual height, runners are then directed off the track onto wet rush towards the Allt Dogha. Briefly on another track, the route crosses the river before runners are directed back off-track over more wet ground. The Allt Dogha is met and crossed once more for a final run down a track to Annat.

With a membership drawn from across the North West Highlands, Lochaber Athletic Club is one of the larger hill-running clubs in Scotland and is a key player in the Scottish hill-running scene. The club hosts a number of major races in the running calendar and organises a Winter League to keep local runners fit outwith the main racing season.

◀ The wet grassy run to the finish (pic: Keith Jeffrey)

Meall Fuar-mhonaidh

Distance 9km Ascent 550m Time allow 1h30 Map OS Landranger 26

Meall Fuar-mhonaidh is a charismatic small hill above the Great Glen with renowned views over Loch Ness. The hill's popularity has created an obvious path which gives an enjoyable run to the summit.

At the south end of the village of Drumnadrochit on Loch Ness, a sign points the way up a dead-end road to Bunloit. Drive up this road and leave vehicles in the car park at the road-end. A sign and wooden post point out the way ahead to the hill or left onto the Great Glen Way. Take the road ahead to a gate with another sign directing you onto an overgrown path between a fence and burn. Some wooden walkways are crossed as the path skirts around a field and arrives at gates across a track. Through the gates and over the track, the path climbs rougher, rooty ground to arrive at yet another gate. Still on the path, a steep ascent through birchwood is followed by a slight levelling out on open heather-clad hillside. The wide path crosses a large deer fence by a stile, before climbing onto Meall Fuar-mhonaidh's northeast shoulder. At a runnable gradient, the undulating crest can be followed for its entire length to the cairns on Meall Fuar-mhonaidh's

summit. In dry weather, the ground is soft underfoot for the most part and encourages a fast ascent. After wet weather, however, many patches of sodden ground prevent direct lines being made between the more solid sections of worn path. Vast views in all directions can be savoured on clear days. Return by the same route.

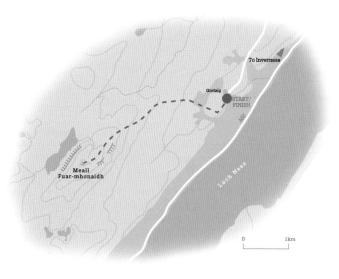

Instead of accessing the foot of this hill by car, it is possible to arrive by bike as the route starts from a point on the Great Glen Cycle Route. At over 120km long, this mainly off-road cycle route runs from Fort William to Inverness, following forestry tracks, the Caledonian Canal towpath and the course of an old railway line. The route has become very popular, but it is worth noting that there are some steep, testing climbs and, when nearing Inverness, sections of road cycling.

◀ Meall Fuar-mhonaidh from near Grotaig

Sgurr an Utha

Distance 6km Ascent 690m Time allow 1h15 Map OS Landranger 40

This small hill is often bypassed for the magnificent peaks that surround Glenfinnan, but it makes for a superb run with spectacular views.

Although Sgurr an Utha sits close to the other higher peaks above Glenfinnan, it is slightly awkwardly placed to include in a long peak-bagging expedition. There is a layby on the A830, 3km west of Glenfinnan, just above the bridge over the Allt an Utha. Park in the layby and head along the road to the bridge, beyond which dense forestry needs to be entered to access the hill. Fortunately, a few metres on from the bridge an opening leads to a fine

track heading northwards. Although this track climbs steeply, the gradient is quite runnable and the forest is quickly left behind. Further on, the track comes to a junction with one fork heading directly ahead via a wooden bridge over the Allt an Utha and the other turning sharp right. To aim for Sgurr an Utha, take the right fork and follow the track as it twists and turns uphill. At around the 320m contour, the track takes an abrupt turn southwards. Leave it at this point and bear northeast on a faint path, crossing wet grassy ground to reach the Allt an Utha. Cross the burn and make a beeline

◄ On Sgurr an Utha looking to Sgurr Thuilm and Streap

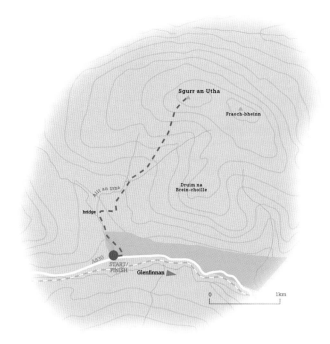

NNE for Sgurr an Utha's summit. Although steep and completely pathless, there are no difficulties ascending the grass- and rush-covered slopes. The climb gives thighs a good workout, and Sgurr an Utha's crest is reached quite quickly. A flat area leads to the foot of the last 50m climb to the rocky summit with its large cairn. The views are simply stunning, particularly considering the little effort expended. A fast downhill run can be enjoyed, retracing the route back to the track or, alternatively, more views can be taken in while running ESE along the wide crest to Fraoch-bheinn and southwestwards returning to the track over Druim na Brein-choille.

119

Beinn Resipol

Distance **14km** Ascent **850m** Time **allow 2h15** Map **OS Landranger 40**

Fine tracks, superb views on clear days and grassy slopes that are a joy to run over – you'll be glad you made the journey into the heart of Sunart for a run up solitary Beinn Resipol.

North of the village of Strontian, the road marked to Polloch is followed for 2km to a junction just beyond a phonebox, where there is limited parking. From the junction, run southwest on the minor road past some houses to a gate. Through the gate, head down a track for 1km to a bridge over the Allt nan Cailleach, beyond which a junction in the track can be seen ahead. Take the right fork to head northwest uphill. Although runnable, the track has been churned over by the local cattle, but conditions underfoot do improve further on after passing some waterworks. After 2km, the track begins to turn northwards aiming for a cairn on the highest point. Before reaching the cairn, leave the track and climb westwards

on the grassy slopes around Beinn a'Chaorainn's northeast shoulder. The ground ahead drops gently to a wide bealach, and a faint path aiming northwest can be picked up to cross the damp, grassy terrain. The path comes and goes as it climbs onto Beinn Resipol's eastern shoulder. Once you gain this, the grassy uphill run with a gentle gradient is a joy. Beyond a lochan, one last uphill pull is required to reach the eastern end of the summit crest and an obvious

path is picked up which leads westwards around crags and rocks to the summit cairn. Return by the same route or, if you can arrange transport, head back to the cairn on Beinn a'Chaorainn's northeast shoulder and run northwards down an overgrown track through forestry to Loch Doilet near Polloch. Refreshments (and accommodation) are available in Strontian and at the Ariundle Centre, passed on the minor road en route to the start.

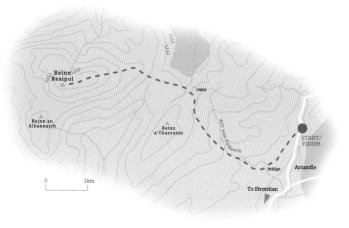

◀ Beinn Resipol from the east

Strathconon ridges

Distance 9km Ascent 985m Time allow 2h Map OS Landranger 25

A pleasant pathless ridge run to gain two Corbetts, with the option of extending the route over two more tops for great views over Strath Bran to the higher peaks to the west.

To the west of Inverness, two narrow roads heading from Contin and Marybank converge and head along Strathconon. Just beyond the village of Milton, the Allt an t-Srathain Mhoir tumbles through forestry to the cottages at Strathanmore. Cars can be parked by some sheep pens, where a large sign welcomes hillwalkers and displays information on the deer management in the area. From a passing place on the road to the south, a faint path can be made out heading up the hill. Follow this path uphill through bracken, heather and rush. As the rate of ascent begins to lessen, the path gradually disappears into the undergrowth. Turn southwest and run towards the crag on Creag Ruadh that can be seen ahead. As the crag is neared, the slope steepens and a faint path starts to form, then continues to the summit. Once on the summit, fine running can be enjoyed aiming northwest along the crest over grass with occasional rocks. A last sharp pull up heather and peat is needed to

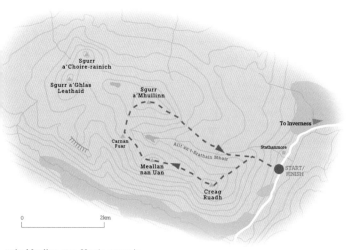

gain Meallan nan Uan's summit. Over more heather and rock, head west, then northwest and drop to a grassy bealach. Carnan Fuar, the minor top ahead, can easily be contoured around on its right-hand side, from where a quick run up a gentle grassy slope leads to Sgurr a'Mhuilinn's broad grass-covered crest. Superb views can be appreciated while sitting by the cairn and the remains of a trig point. Heading southeast, a grassy ridge with several rocky outcrops is run down to reach a flat meadow and the Allt an t-Srathain Mhoir. After crossing the burn, return by the outward route. Although not Corbetts, Sgurr a'Ghlas Leathaid and Sgurr a'Choire-rainich to the northwest can easily be added to the route from Carnan Fuar. These twins give uninterrupted views over Strath Bran to the Fannaichs and Torridon.

A fine example of a Parliamentary Church stands 300m south of the route's start. Designed by Thomas Telford, 32 of these churches were built in remote parts of the Highlands and Islands in the early 19th century, all to the same plan. As a civil engineer, Thomas Telford is credited with vastly improving the Scottish infrastructure through the many significant projects he undertook, including harbours, roads, the Caledonian Canal and 120 bridges in the Highlands.

◀ The western Strathconon Corbett peaks from Loch a'Chroisg

Lochailort Corbetts

Distance **10km** Ascent **1375m** Time **allow 2h30** Map **OS Landranger 40**

Spectacular views are only to be expected from such a magnificent setting in Moidart. This run follows walls and pathless hill crests to gain three Corbetts.

On the A861, 4km southwest of the Lochailort Hotel in Moidart, a tired warning sign on a gate denotes the start of a track through birch forest to a wooden house by Alisary Burn. Head up the track and, just before reaching the house, turn right through a gate to shadow the burn and edge of a forest uphill: the pathless ground can be wet and quite slippery. As the trees come to an end, turn right and head ESE directly uphill over grass and rush. As the terrain levels out, the route

crosses a burn and wall before making a direct ascent of An Stac. Any rocky outcrops are easily bypassed on the left side. Excellent views are to be had from the rocky summit with its small pile of stones. Turn southwards and jog downhill, avoiding a few rocky outcrops. The wall crossed earlier is met again at the bealach above Coire na Cnamha and accompanied over wet, then steeply rising ground to Bealach an Fhiona. Once on the crest of the hill, turn left away from the wall and enjoy a pleasant run along this. Running is easier if you keep to the grass slightly to the south of the crest. The summit cairn on Sgurr na Ba Glaise is quickly reached. Return

◀ An Stac and Rois-Bheinn from Roshven

to Bealach an Fhiona, then follow the wall up the hillside ahead. Grass gives way to more bouldery ground as Rois-Bheinn's summit is neared. A small cairn rests by the wall on the summit. Continue a bit further to the well-constructed cairn on the western top, where uninterrupted views can be savoured. Return to the col between Rois-Bheinn's tops, then aim north and descend steep, loose, grassy ground to eventually meet the outward route by Alisary Burn. In winter, this descent is not recommended as the ground to the north of the col will most likely be iced over; instead return to Bealach an Fhiona and follow the wall back down to Alisary Burn.

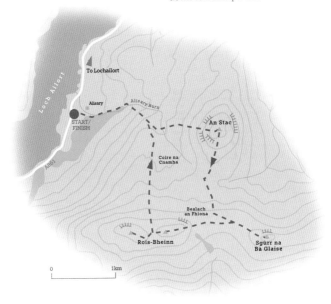

Above Glenelg and Arnisdale

Distance **14km** Ascent **1600m** Time **allow 3h** Map OS Landranger 33

A high-level ridge run with excellent views is the reward for the incredibly steep climb up grass and scree from Arnisdale by Loch Hourn.

Beinn Sgritheall towers above the small village of Arnisdale on the shore of Loch Hourn, which is accessed using the narrow road that twists south from Glenelg. The route starts at the western end of the village, where there is limited parking by the shore; however, more parking is available in a car park nearer the end of the public road. A signpost marks the path to Beinn Sgritheall which initially follows a burn uphill. The path swings east around the line of the houses below and crosses a couple of burns, before turning directly uphill. Following a line of fenceposts, progress is steep but easy and obvious. At around 320m, the path drops slightly to cross a burn, then rises further and splits. Take the left fork, which veers away from the burn and aims directly uphill. Further on, the path gradually disappears into the thick grass before the screes are reached. Keeping to the larger boulders, climb the screes to a small cairn resting on Beinn Sgritheall's eastern bump. Now on runnable grassy terrain, a path is

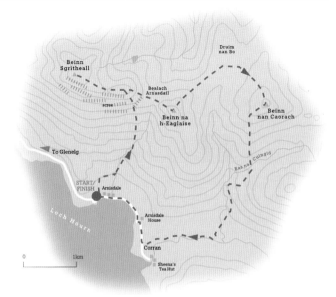

followed westwards to a wide bealach, then northwest uphill. A short, narrow section is easily negotiated and Beinn Sgritheall's ruined trig point is reached shortly thereafter. After returning to the small cairn on the subsidiary summit, descend by a loose path through scree, aiming southeast for Bealach Arnasdail. Aiding navigation in mist, a wall and fenceposts travel up the very steep grass-covered ground ahead to the summit of Beinn na h-Eaglaise. Running northeast along the summit crest, tall fenceposts guide you down to a bealach. Instead

of heading towards Druim nan Bo, you can save height by contouring northeast on pleasant grassy ground. Gradually, the terrain nudges you southeast, aiming directly uphill to Beinn nan Caorach's summit. The easiest return to Arnisdale is southwest for a fast descent to the Eas na Cuingid. On the opposite side of the burn, a stalkers' path is picked up which leads down to a track to return to the road at Corran, 2km from the start. Homebaking and a hot drink can be enjoyed with a blether at Sheena's Tea Hut at the end of the public road.

◀ Glenelg hills from The Saddle

127

Loch Lochy Munros Hill Race

Distance **22km** Ascent **1500m** Category **AL** Records **2:06:36 – Andy Symonds (2009), 2:46:16 – Kate Jenkins (2009)** Time of year **mid-June** Map **OS Landranger 34** Website **www.lochaberac.co.uk**

Some brutal ascents and descents with trail running either side making the most of forestry tracks and paths.

To the west of Spean Bridge, the road crosses the Caledonian Canal at Gairlochy. Some 5km north of the locks, race registration and finish is at Achnacarry. However, the race start is 1km further north on the bridge by the beautiful Eas Chia-aig waterfall in the Dark Mile. After leaving the bridge, the field of runners spread themselves out over 700m of road, then head northeast up a forestry track. This swings northwest and then, in dense forestry, north up Gleann Cia-aig. Where the track ends abruptly, a twisting path takes over, giving technical running over tree roots, rocks and burns. Out of the forest, a fainter path continues to a bridge over the Abhainn Chia-aig, where a wet and indistinct path travels around the base of Meall an Tagraidh to the ruin at Fedden. After using a stile to cross a deer fence, then leaping over a burn, runners need to choose one of the green lines of grass to follow through the otherwise brown heather-clad western slopes of Sron a'Choire

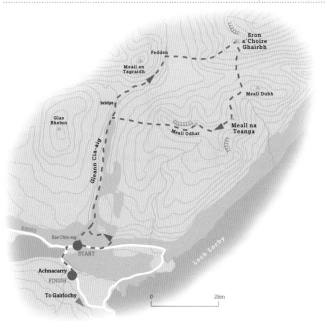

Ghairbh. It's an easy but unrelenting trudge for 500m of ascent. After the summit cairn, the route continues south and descends quite steeply, taking in parts of a stalkers' path to reach a bealach. A path is then picked up to contour around Meall Dubh and reach the col below Meall na Teanga. A stiff ascent is followed by a pleasant run south along Meall na Teanga's crest to the summit cairn, from which it's a drop of 70m southwest to another col and a short climb up to the final summit checkpoint on Meall Coire Lochain. Over Meall Odhar, the ground is grass-covered, making for fairly fast running before the drop on heather-clad slopes to the edge of the forest below. Competitors return though the forest on the path and track used earlier, but turn off the track for a sharp descent by the waterfall onto the road. Now fairly tired, runners will need to hold it together for the last 1km of road running to Achnacarry, where lots of delicious homebaking awaits.

◀ Runners spread out on the ascent up Sron a'Choire Ghairbh

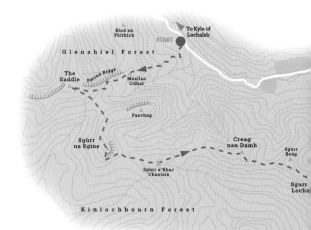

The Saddle and the South Glen Shiel Ridge

Distance 29km Ascent 2750m Time allow 6h30 Map OS Landranger 33

The Saddle, Sgurr na Sgine and the South Glen Shiel Ridge form a classic continuous chain of peaks, giving fast, high-level ridge running on a brilliant day out. Many paths, fenceposts and walls aid navigation on misty days.

Starting near the western end of Glen Shiel, 6km southeast of Shiel Bridge, this long traverse finishes at the Cluanie Inn 15km to the east; therefore, transport ideally needs to be arranged for the return along the road. From a layby 500m southeast of an old quarry, walk southeast

along the road for a further 500m to a gate on the opposite side of the road. An old stalkers' path heads southwards, twisting as it gains height. When the path begins to turn northwest aiming for Biod an Fhithich, leave it and climb over grass directly up the steep eastern shoulder of Meallan Odhar. As the ground levels out, the path is rejoined for a jog to the base of the Forcan Ridge. Although traversing the ridge is considered a classic scramble and not particularly

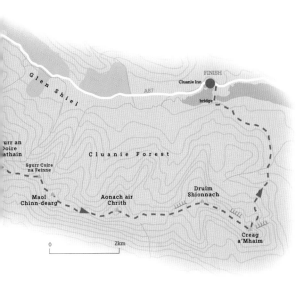

difficult, an easier and quicker route follows a wall heading left. The wall contours around the ridge for 400m, then as it turns south, you leave it to aim west uphill. Join another wall and accompany it to its end, where a steep, loose path rises to The Saddle's summit plateau and its trig point. The top to the northeast is considered the highest point, with fantastic views to Knoydart, Skye, Kintail and further on to Torridon. Return to the top of the wall and look

for a faint path heading slightly right (southeast) towards Bealach Coire Mhalagain. An enjoyable run bounding over the burns and wet, grassy ground comes to a line of fenceposts travelling southeast towards a small lochan. Above the lochan, a faint path veering slightly to the right of the fenceposts and climbing over grass and slabs leads to a fenceline on the wide crest between Sgurr na Sgine and Faochag. Across runnable terrain, follow the fenceposts up to Sgurr na Sgine's flat top with its cairn at the southeast corner. A detour is required to avoid the crags and reach the ground below: turn southwest and run downhill for around 300m, then descend south over grassy ground to another wall, which leads you eastwards towards Bealach an Toiteil, where you join a line of fenceposts to reach Sgurr a'Bhac Chaolais. Beyond the small cairn on this Corbett's summit, follow the fenceposts and wall eastwards to a junction, where keeping left will lead you down to

Bealach Duibh Leac. Here, an obvious path from Glen Shiel, with some posts, guides you eastwards up grassy, undulating ground to Creag nan Damh's summit cairn. It then makes a twisting southeasterly descent to Bealach Fraoch Choire, where a climb begins up towards Sgurr Beag. As this hill is not a Munro, it is often bypassed via a contouring path that begins at a grey metal post, with opportunities to top up water bottles at one of several springs crossing the path on the way. Bealach a'Choire Reidhe is gained next, with the summit of

Sgurr an Lochain less than 500m away, up a worn path. Beyond here, the path bears southeast and drops to Bealach Sgurr an Lochain, where posts continue towards Sgurr an Doire Leathain with views opening up over Loch Quoich to the Rough Bounds of Knoydart behind. As this hill's crest is attained, the route turns northeast away from the posts for a 200m detour to its summit cairn. Retrace your steps along the crest to rejoin the posts and follow them southeastwards down to Bealach Caol na Droma Moire. Like Sgurr Beag earlier, the next peak, Sgurr Coire na Feinne, is not a Munro and so it is often bypassed in favour of a more direct line to Bealach Caol na Droma Bige and Maol Chinn-dearg beyond. Some superb running along the undulating crest is enjoyed on the worn path to Aonach air Chrith. Dropping southeast from Aonach air Chrith, a wide flat grassy col is gained which turns east for a gentle climb to a plateau. The path fades and is easily lost in mist on the stretch to Druim Shionnach, so it is worth noting that the first cairn reached on this hill does not mark the summit. The summit is a couple of minutes further on, resting above Coire nan Leac where the deer rutt loudly in August and September. Now very narrow, the ridge continues east from Druim Shionnach, with care needed as the path crosses from one side of the ridge to the other and back again. The ridge begins to widen out before reaching the last col. With a bit of effort, a short run up the obvious path leads to the large cairn on Creag a'Mhaim. Now at the end of the ridge, some time should be taken to appreciate the stunning views in all directions. A fine stalkers' path heads southeast to the old road, which you turn left onto and follow northwards back to the A87. However, by retracing your steps for a few metres from the cairn, a faint path takes a more direct route north. On this option, the initial section is steep but runnable, dropping over grassy ground into Coirean an Eich Bhric. More gentle slopes are then crossed while running through ever-thickening heather. A deer fence is crossed, with a last wet run to reach the bridge on the old road, where a 3km run awaits for the return to the A87 at the Cluanie Inn.

The Mullardoch circuit

Distance **55km** Ascent **4950m** Time **allow 14 hours**
Map **OS Landranger 25**

Above Loch Mullardoch are 12 Munros that
form a great long-distance running route
along a circuit of high ridges and crests.
Taking in spectacular scenery, this is a major
undertaking and should be attempted outwith
winter to maximise daylight on the journey.
Although not a time challenge in the vein
of Ramsay's Round, the fastest recorded
time is by Alec Keith in just 10 hours
and 24 minutes!

A narrow road heads west from
Cannich in Strathglass and ends at
Mullardoch Dam. Loch Mullardoch
was dammed in 1952 and with no
tracks or roads having since been
built to replace those flooded, the
area feels very isolated. There is,
however, plenty of space for
parking either side of the dam.
The route is best done in an
anticlockwise direction, leaving
the thick heather in Fraoch-
choire for the end of the
day. Beginning on a track
at the northern end of
the dam, head down to
a boathouse and the
Chisholm Stone, then
climb westwards
through heather. The
track narrows to a path
and comes to a bridge
over the Allt Mullardoch.

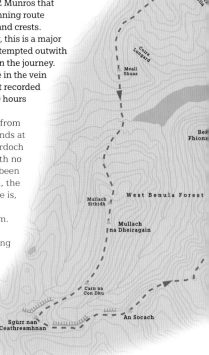

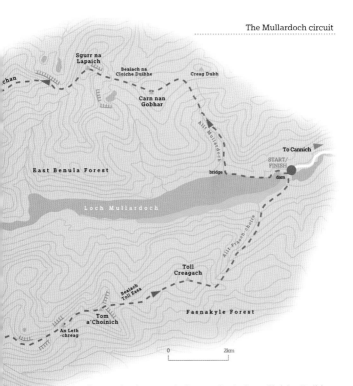

Sgurr na Lapaich
Bealach na Cloiche Duibhe
Creag Dubh
chan
Carn nan Gobhar
East Benula Forest
To Cannich
START/FINISH
Allt Mullardoch
bridge
dam
Loch Mullardoch
Allt Fraoch-choire
Toll Creagach
Bealach Toll Easa
Tom a'Choinich
Fasnakyle Forest
An Leth-chreag
0   2km

Instead of crossing here, take the northbound path on the east bank, stepping over the burn after 2km to climb heathery, virtually pathless ground to the bealach between Creag Dubh and Carn nan Gobhar. Run west over pleasant grass-covered terrain to Carn nan Gobhar's two cairns resting on its bouldery summit. On a faint path, which picks its way initially through some boulderfields, run down to a small

lochan on Bealach na Cloiche Duibhe. The path becomes more obvious as it begins to wind its way up steep grass, then boulders and rocks to attain Sgurr na Lapaich. Run southwest downhill over grass to the bealach, then follow a path uphill, twisting on a narrow section of the crest, to reach a tidy cairn marking the start of An Riabhachan's long, wide crest. A delightful 750m run over grassy ground gains the main

135

summit cairn. From a cairn some 1500m further along the crest, a loose path drops northwest to a narrow col. A minor top is easily bypassed on the left, thereafter a path is taken down to windy Bealach Bholla. The path continues steeply uphill to reach a minor top on An Socach's east arm, with the summit trig point a short distance further on. West of An Socach, there are no paths but the grass-covered ground is a joy to run over. Leave the summit and drop southwest to the wide curving crest above Coire Lungard, which is followed to Meall Shuas. A quick descent is enjoyed while bounding down the thick grass and rush to reach the river to the west of Loch Mullardoch. After crossing the river and a track to the south, climb a vague path which follows the west side of the Allt Cam to a waterfall. The path disappears into the wet grass thereafter, and it's a bit of a trudge to gain Mullach Sithidh. Now on a runnable crest aiming southwest, traverse a narrow bealach to reach Mullach na Dheiragain. Over a wide grassy crest, a path bears south to the next bealach, then ascends the narrowing

hill ahead to gain the flat, boulder-covered plateau of Carn na Con Dhu. After picking a route through and around the boulders, the path descends to another bealach, before climbing a steep and narrowing crest to reach Sgurr nan Ceathreamhnan's small summit with its untidy cairn. A worn path, initially bearing southeast, continues for 3km along a crest and over several minor tops to a grassy, wet rise, from which An Socach with its large cairn is attained. To the northeast cross a minor summit and drop down to a wide grassy col, before picking up a stalkers' path to climb the hillside ahead. After a climb to gain around 300m in height, where the path fades and begins to turn to contour northwards, leave the path and continue northeast onto the gravel-covered crest of Mam Sodhail's southwest shoulder, running along this past the remains of a building to the summit shortly after. Here, you'll find a huge cairn which gives good shelter from the wind. Bear north on a worn path to drop to the next bealach, then contour around Carn Eige on grassy ground. Water bottles can be topped up at a spring on the way, before descending to the wide, grassy col below Beinn Fhionnlaidh. An obvious path travels to the summit with its

well-constructed cairn and fine views along Loch Mullardoch. Return to the col and trudge up a distinct path to the small pile of rocks on Carn Eige's summit, then jog east down to a wide grass-covered plateau. Some fenceposts are picked up and, further on, the crest turns southeast with the path winding between rocky outcrops. The crest then widens and the path follows occasional fenceposts and scree over Sron Garbh, An Leth-chreag and Tom a'Choinich Beag for a grassy pull to the summit of Tom a'Choinich. The path gives a steep, twisting descent to Bealach Toll Easa, then rises eastwards by more fenceposts to a grassy plateau. This is quickly crossed, and one final gentle ascent over grass gains Toll Creagach's summit. Now with tiring legs, the easiest though not most direct return to the dam begins by heading east and dropping to a wide grassy col. From the col, turn northeast and, keeping east of the Allt Fraoch-choire, cross grass and heather towards the dam. The heather does get thicker further down but, nearing the dam, a faint path can be picked up aiming you through fences and down steps to some hydro buildings above the loch. A last jog down the road ends up back at the start.

◂ Looking west from Tom a'Choinich towards Carn Eige

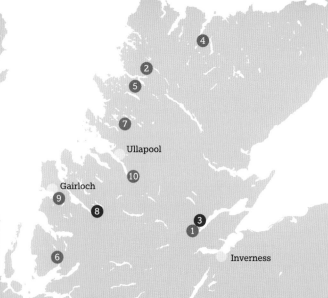

Ullapool

Gairloch

Inverness

Wild and remote, the Northern Highlands provide some of the country's most challenging hill runs. Being sparsely populated, however, there are few organised hill races. The Knockfarrel and Cioch Mhor Hill Races are fairly short, yet the terrain in forest and on overgrown paths presents testing obstacles for competitors. The peaks of Ben Stack and Ben Loyal are straightforward to ascend, and both give vast views for surprisingly little effort. Running over the Corbett peaks on Quinag is easier than expected: just stop occasionally to take in the views over the cliffs and buttresses. More Corbett-bagging is to be enjoyed in Applecross and Drumrunie Forest,

but these routes have slightly stiffer ascents and rougher terrain. The Slioch Horseshoe Hill Race seems to have a habit of taking place on one of the hottest days of the year, but the effort is rewarded by great-tasting homebaking at the finish. A long track enables fast running and easy access into Flowerdale Forest, where two grass-covered Corbetts that sit either side of Loch na h-Oidhche can be climbed in a circular route. The longest route in this chapter is in the remote region southeast of Ullapool and, although good tracks and old stalkers' paths aid progress into the area, navigation skills will be tested throughout the day, even in clear conditions.

Northern Highlands

Knockfarrel Hill Race

Distance 8km Ascent 350m Category BS Records 37:24 – Graeme Bartlett (2000), 43:20 – Tracey Brindley (2004) Time of year early April
Map OS Landranger 26 Website www.highlandhillrunners.org.uk

Don't let the figures fool you, this is a tough little hill race! Although mainly on tracks and paths, the heather, thistles and gorse will scar even the hardiest of legs.

The race starts from the old station in Strathpeffer at the end of the now disused railway spur from Dingwall. Runners head eastwards along the old railway line for 600m, now much overgrown, worn and mucky. Through a gate, the route turns southeast and starts climbing up a field on a rough path to a stile. Now on a path travelling up a narrow fenced gap between fields, competitors' bodies twist and turn as they try to avoid being scratched by the gorse and thistles. Arriving at another stile, the route then turns northeast and continues along a rough, overgrown track with fallen trees for 700m. Runners are directed south and scramble up a very steep,

wet slope towards Knockfarrel's summit. From the summit, the route travels on a path aiming southwest along the hill's crest for just over 1km. A section of track is briefly followed, then a run on a fainter path through heather is enjoyed up to Cnoc Mor's summit. About-turning, runners drop northwards into the forest for a fast descent to a track that returns them to the stile at the top of the path with the gorse and thistles. Competitors retrace their steps back to the station.

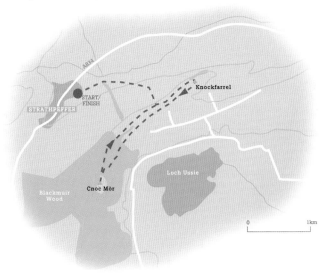

Knockfarrel Hill Race dates back to the 1960s and was set up by Ross-shire SAC. Due to various circumstances, the race organisation and route changed a few times over the years and is now managed by Highland Hillrunners. The original winners' trophy was examined in the early 1980s and found not to be of the inferior plated type but to be solid silver!

◄ Knockfarrel's summit in sight (pic: Paul Matheson, Highland Hillrunners)

Ben Stack

Distance **7km** Ascent **700m** Time **allow 1h30** Map **OS Landranger 9**

Schiehallion-esque in shape, this little hill sits alone above a lochan-pitted landscape in remote Sutherland. Grass-covered terrain and straightforward navigation make for an enjoyable and quick hill run.

On the A838, just south of Loch Stack, a track crosses the inflow to the loch and continues in the direction of Arkle, Meall Horn and Foinaven. Park at the access to this track and walk south along the road to the next passing place. From the west side of the road, head northwest along a short section of rough track which crosses damp ground. The track gives way to a faint path which can be jogged over uphill until it eventually disappears into the grass at around the 350m contour. Thereafter, aim northwest up a runnable gradient over grass and between gneiss humps to a minor summit at around 540m, where a path appears and shows the route ahead to the main summit. The rate of climbing steepens for the remaining 200m of ascent. Ben

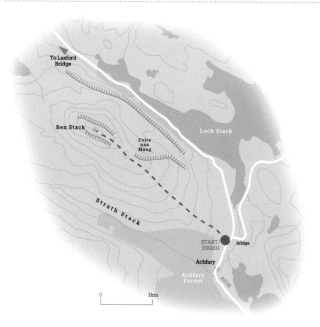

Stack's summit crest is split along its length by a landslip, and the summit point is the westerly cairn and not the trig point. An aerial with solar power has been erected close to the cairn. The views are outstanding, with the mountains of Foinaven, Meall Horn and Arkle shown in detail. Return downhill by the same route.

Foinaven to the north of Ben Stack has been subject to serious debate over the last two decades. In 1993, its summit Ganu Mor was given a spot height of 915m and the mountain was, therefore, promoted to Munro status. The local hotels braced themselves for an influx of Munro-baggers. It wasn't until 2007 that the debate was finally put to rest when the Munro Society commissioned a surveying company to measure the height using sophisticated GPS equipment. Its height now stands at 911m. The bulk of this vast mountain is covered in quartzite boulders, which make for a very unrunnable day, particularly when wet.

◀ Ben Stack from the west

Cioch Mhor Hill Race

Distance 14km Ascent 680m Category AM Records 1:08:18 – Alec Keith (2009),
1:29:47 – Roxy Bannerman (2009) Time of year mid-April
Maps OS Landranger 20 and 21 Website www.highlandhillrunners.org.uk

With fields of grass and livestock to cross, and bog and heather to wade through, this race is tougher than it initially appears on the map. With only the summits as checkpoints, good route choice is essential – so it helps to follow a local!

Tulloch Castle Hotel is at the northern end of Dingwall, and signs along the town's main road enable the castle to be easily found. The race sets off from behind the hotel and heads east uphill along a farm track. After an abrupt turn through a wall, runners are directed onto grazing land to bear northwards. Further uphill, a couple of gates need crossing, then a faint trod can be found to follow to the trig point on Cnoc a'Bhreacaich. Turning northwest beyond the trig point, grass, heather and tussocks are bounded over to reach the damp ground below at Bog a'Bhreacaich. After negotiating a fence, crossing the burn and leaping over more tussocks a track is met which can be followed uphill for 1km until a stile is

◄ On the Cioch Mhor Hill Race (pic: Highland Hillrunners)

seen on the adjacent fence. This stile marks where runners should leave the track and plod through deep heather over the short distance to Cioch Mhor's summit. The return is by the same route, though locals are happy to share advice on faster route variants.

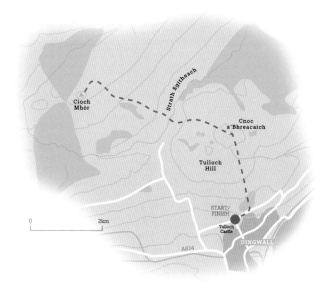

Highland Hillrunners club was formed in 1991 and their running colours were originally light blue. Scottish Athletics demanded a colour change, so a yellow and green combination was chosen. This proved so unpopular with the club that it was replaced by dark blue with a tartan stripe, which has now become one of the most instantly recognisable vests on the hills.

Ben Loyal

Distance 10km Ascent 775m Time allow 1h45 Map OS Landranger 10

The 'Queen of Scottish Peaks' has an imposing figure when viewed from the north and west with its four granite tors. The forgotten eastern side, however, gives great running up a gentle grass-covered incline.

On the western shore of Loch Loyal, 2.5km north of Loch Loyal Lodge, a bridge over a burn indicates the start of this route up Ben Loyal. Faint traces of path can be found, otherwise the ground is covered in short grass and rush with occasional moss, making for an enjoyable run. Past a circular shieling, the main summit tor, An Caisteal, can be seen directly ahead. For the first 2km of the route, simply make a beeline for this tor. The ground thereafter steepens and becomes heather clad, though never too thickly. At this point begin to turn northwest, aiming for hidden Loch na Creige Riabhaich. Upon reaching the lochan, skirt around it, then up more grass-covered hillside onto Ben

Loyal's crest. Turn north and, now on a path, follow the crest to Sgor Chaonasaid to obtain uninterrupted views north and to Orkney. About-turn and run along the crest over delightful grass past Sgor a'Bhatain and up An Caisteal. A short scramble is needed to attain the summit with its hidden trig point and vast panoramas. To descend An Caisteal, retrace the route for a few metres, then pick up the path on the western edge of the crest and head south over more pleasant grass to Beinn Bheag. A wonderful fast descent can be had by aiming due east from this minor top down steep grass and rush. As the ground flattens out, beware of occasional moss-topped bogs as you run back to the road.

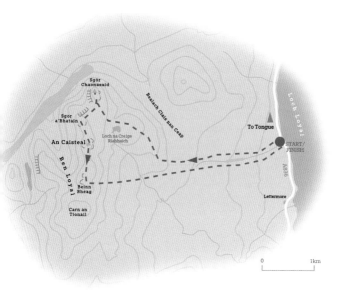

◂ Ben Loyal from the Kyle of Tongue

147

Quinag

Distance **13km** Ascent **1150m** Time allow **2h30** Map **OS Landranger 15**

An iconic mountain gives surprisingly easy running along crests. The views from the summits, ridges and outlying spurs are awesome and vast.

Around 1km south of the highest point on the A894 and 3km north of the junction with the A837, there is a car park. On the opposite side of the road a bridge crosses the Allt Sgiathaig, beyond which an old stalkers' path heads uphill. Initially take this path, leaving it shortly after to branch left on a faint path rising through the heather and over some rocky slabs to join the southeast crest of Spidean Coinich. Ascend a minor top at around the 620m contour, drop over bouldery ground to a small lochan, then climb steeply to Spidean Coinich's summit. An obvious path drops to a small bealach with a lochan, then climbs over a minor summit to descend steep grassy ground to Bealach a'Chornaidh. Ahead is a minor summit (marked 745m), which a twisting path steeply ascends. At the next col northwest beyond this, there are some interesting crags and rocky ledges off left. The path climbs up and around the east side of the next bump before a gradual, runnable ascent of Sail Ghorm with wonderful views. Return to the col just before the summit at 745m,

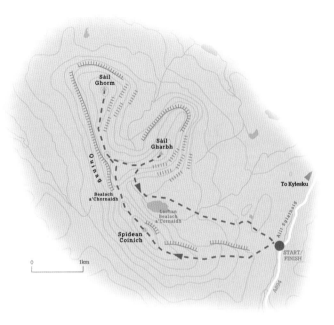

then contour on the grass-covered slopes to the left – beware, some of the ground is very loose. Ahead the route to Sail Gharbh is obvious. The pink sandstone dramatically gives way to grey quartzite capping the summit crest, with superb views in all directions from the summit cairn and trig point. Return along the crest, looking for a small cairn off left which marks a rough path down towards Bealach a'Chornaidh and Lochan Bealach Cornaidh below. Easy running with fine views towards Conival is enjoyed for the return to the car park.

Below Quinag to the north, Kylesku Bridge crosses a narrow stretch of seawater. Replacing the free ferry in 1984, this multi-award winning bridge curves beautifully above the water from Kylesku to the northern shore, where a car park and viewpoint give a spectacular panorama of the Quinag peaks.

◀ Sail Gharbh from Spidean Coinich's eastern shoulder

Applecross Corbetts

Distance 14km **Ascent** 1350m **Time** allow 2h45 **Map** OS Explorer 428

A superb high-level run on wide crests alongside dramatic drops into dark coires. Amazing views in all directions, including a full-frontal of Skye's Cuillin.

The route start and finish are 6km apart, so it's a good idea to leave a bike or road trainers at the route end for the returning descent on road. Start by the bridge over Russel Burn on the Bealach na Ba road, branching off the A896 northwest of Lochcarron. Immediately head north on a rough track. As it levels out, leave the track, turn northeast and run over wet grass to reach the base of Beinn Bhan's southern shoulder. A climb over heather gains this shoulder, where the terrain changes to runnable grass with occasional rocks and boulders. Heading northwards, a path gradually forms as height is gained. On reaching a subsidiary top, dramatic A'Chioch and Coire na Feola – with its precipitous drops – come into view. Further on Beinn Bhan's wide, flat summit plateau sits above east-facing corries with dark lochans. A summit trig point is well sheltered in its stone circle. Turn west and leave the grass behind to jog over

Bealach na Ba used to be the only road connection Applecross had with the outside world. This narrow, twisting route climbs to over 600m (2000 feet) and is frequently blocked in winter. A sign at the road start informs road users of this and discourages learner drivers, large vehicles and caravans from proceeding further. It wasn't until 1975 that Applecross was connected to Shieldaig via a more reliable but less fun coastal road.

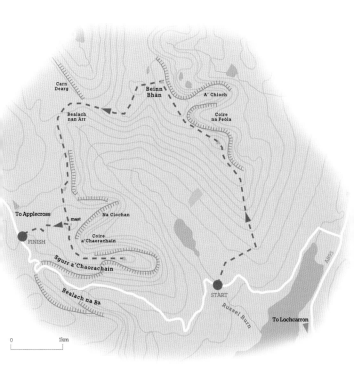

complex boulder-strewn crests to Bealach nan Arr. Bypass Carn Dearg using a faint path contouring through heather to the next bealach. On more boulder-covered ground, head south up to the mast on Sgurr a'Chaorachain's northern summit. The view to Skye's Cuillin is uninterrupted and stunning. Now mainly on grass, follow an indistinct path above and around Coire a'Chaorachain to the hill's main summit with its fine view onto the Na Ciochan buttress with its angled sandstone terraces. Return to the mast, then descend the track to the car park.

◀ Looking along Sgurr a'Chaorachain towards the Cuillin on Skye

151

Cul Beag and Cul Mor

Distance 14.5km Ascent 1650m Time allow 3h30 Map OS Landranger 15

Grass-covered summits and a beautiful 'lost valley' are gained by using old stalkers' paths and easy green lines up steep heathery slopes.

To gain both Cul Beag and Cul Mor, start on an old stalkers' path rising behind some old trees, 2km east of the main Stac Pollaidh car park in Inverpolly Nature Reserve. Follow the path to its highest point, just above Lochan Fhionnlaidh, then head east aiming for some green lines in the otherwise brown heather-clad hillside. As the incline steepens, a path forms, which winds its way up to a small dip in Cul Beag's northern spur. Upon reaching this dip, turn south and follow the path to Cul Beag's grass-covered summit with precipitous drops to the west and superb views over Ben More Coigach. Return to the dip, running down the loose gravel, then turn northeast along more grass lines which enable a fine, fast descent through the heather. Aim for the outflow of Lochan Dearg, cross it, then climb northwards over steep grass and through a few ferns to reach Lochan Dearg a'Chuil Mhoir. This lochan is central to a wonderful 'lost valley' and has a soft beach with

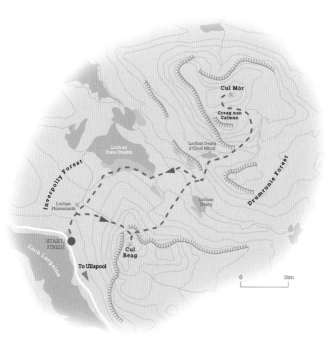

intriguing views to Stac Pollaidh. Bear northeast, aiming for a gap in the sandstone outcrops, then continue around the back of Creag nan Calman. The heather gives way to delightful short grass at around the 650m contour, making for an easy ascent up to the cairn on Cul Mor and stunning views over Suilven. To return, run back down the grass and heather towards Lochan Dearg's outflow. Below, ignore what appears to be a track heading northwest and instead aim west to meet up with the faint path following Loch an Doire Dhuibh's southern shore. Continue through a natural forest, beyond which the path improves and inclines gently up to Lochan Fhionnlaidh. From there, retrace your steps to the road.

◀ Cul Mor from Stac Pollaidh

153

Slioch Horseshoe Hill Race

Distance 19km Ascent 1300m Category AL Records 2:10:23 – Brian Marshall (2009), 2:28:40 – Claire Whitehead (2009) Time of year late May
Map OS Landranger 19 Website www.highlandhillrunners.org.uk

A challenging race up an imposing Munro in a dramatic location. Plenty of burns and lochans cool down runners in a race that has traditionally taken place in hot weather.

Starting from the car park at Incheril, which is up a narrow road just to the east of Kinlochewe, the route heads along a well-defined path through the grass fields by the cemetery. After crossing the Allt Chnaimhean via a wooden bridge, the route continues for 3km, popping in and out of woods to arrive at the bridge over the Abhainn an Fhasaigh. Turning abruptly northeast, the runners cross a burn and meet a small cairn marking a junction in the path. The route takes the left fork on a rising course, where runners clamber up rocks aside a burn. At around the 400m contour, the path is left behind and replaced by a very stiff climb up

Although Highland Hill Runners organise many hill races, they have come unstuck when trying to organise races over some classic mountains including Beinn Dearg, The Saddle, and the Five Sisters of Kintail. When attempting to set up a new race in 2008, Ben Wyvis was initially suggested. However, due to the presence of rare plants, Scottish Natural Heritage (SNH) refused permission and Slioch was put forward instead. Slioch's landowner was for it, but the bridge over the Abhainn an Fhasaigh had to be replaced. Luckily SNH came forward with some money and the Slioch Hill Race was born.

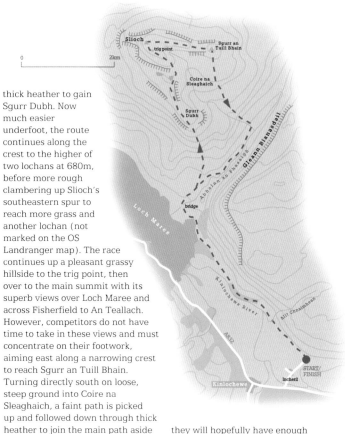

thick heather to gain Sgurr Dubh. Now much easier underfoot, the route continues along the crest to the higher of two lochans at 680m, before more rough clambering up Slioch's southeastern spur to reach more grass and another lochan (not marked on the OS Landranger map). The race continues up a pleasant grassy hillside to the trig point, then over to the main summit with its superb views over Loch Maree and across Fisherfield to An Teallach. However, competitors do not have time to take in these views and must concentrate on their footwork, aiming east along a narrowing crest to reach Sgurr an Tuill Bhain. Turning directly south on loose, steep ground into Coire na Sleaghaich, a faint path is picked up and followed down through thick heather to join the main path aside the Abhainn an Fhasaigh to return to the bridge. If runners are not completely exhausted by this point,

they will hopefully have enough energy to run back to the finish where a great spread of homebaking and sandwiches awaits.

◀ Heading up Sgurr Dubh, Beinn a'Mhuinidh beyond

155

Flowerdale Forest

Distance 23km Ascent 1575m Time allow 4h Map OS Landranger 19

Fine running is had along a rough track that leads to Loch na h-Oidhche, above which towers the long grass-covered crest of Beinn an Eoin and the complex coires of Baosbheinn.

On the A832, 7km southeast of Gairloch, an old green hut and parking area indicate the start of this route. On the opposite side of the road, a wooden shelter and noticeboard stand beside a bridge over the outflow to Am Feur-Loch. Cross this bridge and head down the track. The OS maps suggest a path, but it is, in fact, a rough track which is rideable by mountain bike. Jog

down the track for 4km to a gate, go through it, cross the Abhainn Loch na h-Oidhche and, after 300m or so, the ground begins to level out. Leave the track here and aim for the left of the cliffs ahead. The ground steepens, but there are no difficulties clambering up the heather. As the ascent becomes gradually more gentle, the heather gives way to grass and occasional boulders and running along the crest becomes enjoyable, particularly with a northwesterly wind behind. Eventually Beinn an Eoin's summit is approached with its stunning views

◄ The Grouse Stone and Beinn an Eoin

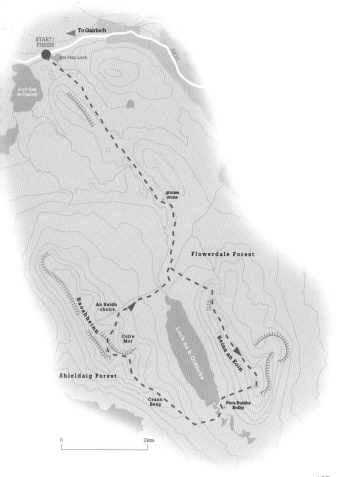

START/
FINISH

To Gairloch

Am Feur-Loch

A832

Loch Bad
an Sgalaig

grouse
stone

Flowerdale Forest

Baosbheinn

An Reidh
-choire

Coire
Mor

Loch na h-Oidhche

Beinn an Eoin

Shieldaig Forest

Ceann
Beag

Poca Buidhe
Bothy

0   2km

▲ On Beinn an Eoin's summit ridge

over the neighbouring Torridon peaks and its unique aspect of Coire Mhic Fhearchair in Beinn Eighe. Return along the ridge for around 200m, then drop WSW directly down to the southern end of Loch na h-Oidhche below. Cross the wet heather and moss, then start trudging westwards uphill through heather. Higher up, both subsidiary tops preceding Baosbheinn's main summit can be bypassed to cut down on the ascent. From Baosbheinn's main summit, head northwards, dropping down delightful, gentle grass-covered slopes to reach An Reidh-choire, then cross heather and moss to meet the track near the point at which you left it. Retrace the route along the track to the road.

The Grouse Stone seen by the gate on the track is an 'erratic' dumped by glaciers in the last ice age. This particular stone is where a shooting party's ghillie would leave a bag containing the day's shot grouse. The ghillie would return to rejoin his party and another ghillie would travel up from Gairloch to collect the bag for the estate's larder.

On Seana Bhraigh looking towards Coigach ▶

Inverlael Munros

Distance **35km** Ascent **2550m** Time allow **8h** Map OS Landranger 20

Confusing forestry tracks lead into a vast wilderness with stunning scenery and interesting topography to test navigation skills.

Start from the new car park at Inverlael, 10km south of Ullapool on the A835, and take a track east into forest. Some 2km further on, veer left and cross the River Lael, then head up the track. Keep left at the sign for Beinn Dearg, then left again at another junction in the tracks. The track fizzles out and an old stalking path takes over, carries on through a gate and leaves the forestry behind. Keeping to the path, follow it for 4km into Coire an Lochain Sgeirich, then another 2km around the southern base of Meall Glac an Ruighe. As the path turns southeast towards a cairn, leave it and bear eastwards over pathless terrain to reach a lochan at 750m. Drop northeast to the head of Cadha Dearg, then climb over grass-covered ground, passing the top of a waterfall and around the summit marked 906m, aiming directly up to

Seana Bhraigh. After the grassy slog up this hill's southeast arm, beautiful Luchd Choire and craggy Creag an Duine come as quite a surprise. The views are vast and far-reaching. Return to the lochan at 750m, then head directly up grass and occasional boulders to Eididh nan Clach Geala. Two cairns sit on the summit plateau with a small dip between. Aim southeast down grassy escarpments to the bealach before Meall nan Ceapraichean. Turn south and start ascending pathless wet ground to Ceann Garbh, which steepens further up. Once on the crest, bypass a slight rise and aim directly for Meall nan Ceapraichean's cairn on its boulder-covered top. Bear southeast on a faint path to a bealach with several lochans, then

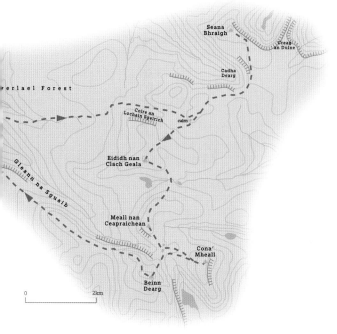

east over a minor bump (marked 886m) to drop to a slightly wet bealach. A faint path can be seen ahead, picking a route through the boulderfields above to reach the long narrow summit of Cona'Mheall with drops to the east. From the summit, return to the bealach and contour around the southern side of the bump to meet up with the Destitution Wall near the lochans: the wall was built by starving labourers in exchange for food during the famine of the 1840s. Aiming southwest, follow the wall uphill, scrambling in bits, to a broken gap where the wall turns sharply west. Beinn Dearg's summit and its huge cairn lie 100m or so south of here. Return to the wall and follow it westwards until it abruptly ends. Drop down ever-steepening heather-clad ground into Gleann na Sguaib, cross the River Lael and pick up the path to re-enter the forest and return to Inverlael.

◀ Heading up Eididh nan Clach Geala, Creag an Duine distant

LEWIS

NORTH HARRIS ④

NORTH UIST ①

② SOUTH UIST

SKYE

⑨

Portree

③ ⑥

Craignure

⑧ ⑦

MULL

JURA

⑩

ISLAY

ARRAN ⑤

Scotland's island groups are individually distinct, thus their hills and mountain ranges have very different characters. Northern Arran is a magnet to hillwalkers, scramblers and climbers alike and Goatfell, the island's highest peak, has a tourist path to the summit, making it ideal for running up and down. Jura's rugged scree-clad skyline is attained in a tough race which is the centrepiece of a hill runners' weekend of socialising and catching up. In Mull, the high screes of Ben More and its neighbours dominate the landscape above Loch na Keal and make for a tough hill race, whereas a fine track up Dun da Ghaoithe gives quick access to the summit over grassy slopes. Skye's David Shepherd Memorial Glamaig Hill Race and Beinn na Caillich circuit offer some of the finest scree running available, whereas the Trotternish Ridge to the north gives running over grassy terrain through some of the country's weirdest rock formations. The Ben Lee Hill Race in North Uist and Ben Kenneth Hill Race in South Uist are events not to be missed and often occur on the same weekend, both requiring water crossings. Clisham in Harris is the highest peak in the Outer Hebrides and, with fine off-path hill running, requires surprisingly little effort to reach the summit with its stunning views.

The Islands

Ben Lee Hill Race and Walk

Distance 8.5km Ascent 330m Category BS Records 41:35 – Jon Duncan (2002),
53:45 – Kate Jenkins (2003) Time of year first Friday in August
Map OS Landranger 18

Unforgiving heathery climbs, a rocky crest, undulating wet ground and a 3km road run to the finish results in a hill race much more challenging than the category suggests.

From Lochmaddy Pier in North Uist, a fast coastguard boat ferries runners over the bay to the foot of Ben Lee (Li a'Tuath). The well-marked race begins by a fenceline, from where runners head up damp tussocky ground. As the ground rises, the route leaves the fence, crosses heather and aims for a green bank travelling below some crags. Though steep, this bank is grassy and easy to climb. As the ascent begins to ease, markers point right for a brief scramble up over some rock. After reaching some bits of wreckage from a B24 bomber that crashed into the hill in 1943, the route turns south up grass and rock to reach Ben Lee's summit trig point. The route is then flagged southwest along the hill's crest to a small dip, where runners aim west up a grassy strip and onto rock higher up to attain Ben Lee's southwest summit. Following markers, a steep heathery descent is made northwest to a fenceline. At a marked point, runners cross the fence and shadow another fence over wet, tussocky ground towards Loch Nighe. On the approach to the loch, the fence turns abruptly right: contestants need to look directly ahead for a flagged gate

◄ Competitors being taken to the race start from Lochmaddy

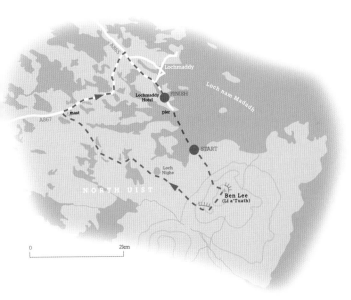

in another fenceline, partially hidden by the rising ground. Flags mark faint trods through the heather and over the moorland, but the evening sun may obscure the markers, making route finding tricky. Aiming generally left of a mast that can be seen ahead, runners have a last drop to yet another fenceline, with the barbed wire taped over at a marked crossing. One last slight rise over grassy ground is required to reach the highest point on the road to the west of the mast. Competitors then endure 3km of road running back to Lochmaddy Hotel.

Instead of racing, the flagged route can be enjoyed at a more leisurely pace. Starting at the same point, but transported across the bay 30 minutes earlier, walkers can savour the views to Harris, South Uist and Skye as they plod over the route. In the evening a ceilidh is held in the local village hall.

Ben Kenneth Hill Race

Distance 5-8km (depending on route choice) Ascent 300m Category BS
Records 33:00 – Ronald MacDonald (1987), 49:14 – Kerry MacPhee (2003)
Time of year first Sunday in August Map OS Landranger 31
Website www.ianbinnie.me.uk

This run up Ben Kenneth, or Beinn Ruigh Choinnich, is a hill race with a long history and a slightly novel way for runners to refresh themselves.

Devised in 1970 to keep the young people of South Uist on the right track, the Ben Kenneth Hill Race starts from Lochboisdale Pier, where contestants run up the village's main street for 400m, then turn right towards the post office. Behind the post office, a fairly new foot causeway is crossed and runners are presented with a choice of turning left or right. Those who don't want to get wet should turn left at the end of the causeway, pick up a road and turn right at the end of it to head across a bridge over the Loch a'Bharp outflow. Alternatively,

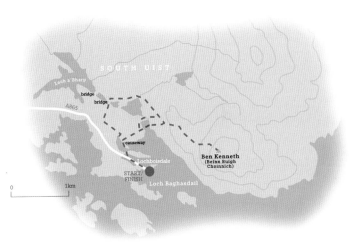

runners can turn right at the end of the causeway, cross a fence and run between two houses, then either head slightly upstream and wade across the shallow channel by a pipe, taking care not to slip onto the sharp barnacles or, if aiming for a fast time, swim directly across the narrow but deeper channel ahead, where seaweed and a current will conspire to inhibit progress. Coastguard boats are in attendance at both water crossings. Onto the other side, a faint path can be followed by all runners to a fenceline with a gate to jump over. Thereafter, the path continues uphill through

the heather to some marshals on a minor top. A flat section is next, then the gradient steepens sharply for the last pull to the summit cairn resting on rocky slabs. Competitors run around the cairn and aim back to Lochboisdale, trying not to get lost in the heather, ferns and nettles on approaching the channel. Upon entering the main street, runners are greeted by a large crowd of cheering spectators and much sounding of car horns. At the prizegiving later in the evening, every finisher is rewarded with a unique hand-crafted souvenir and certificate of the race.

◄ Runners after swimming back over the channel

David Shepherd Memorial Glamaig Hill Race

Distance **6km** Ascent **775m** Category **AS** Records **44:41 – Mark Rigby (1997), 56:10 – Trish Calder (1990)** Time of year **July** Map **OS Landranger 32** Website **www.carnethy.com**

The Glamaig Hill Race is notorious for its steep scree and boulder descent. It is, however, a great spectator event and, combined with the post-race meal, drink and ceilidh, has become a highlight in the hill racing calendar.

The Glamaig Hill Race starts from Skye's Sligachan Hotel and follows a flagged route over the old bridge and along the road for a few metres to a gate. Beyond the gate, runners are free to choose any route they wish to the summit. There is, however, a faint wet path that can be followed through the heather and across the bogs to reach the foot of Glamaig. Runners can then climb directly uphill, initially on steep grass-covered slopes. Gradually, loose rock and scree take over; however, a grassy line higher up and slightly to the left of a direct ascent can make progress more straightforward. After one last pull on a path through scree,

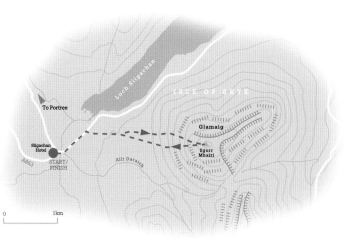

Glamaig's summit is attained and contestants run around the cairn. To return, the path back down through the scree is followed for a short distance, then as this begins to pull right, those runners with strong ankles and a fearless disposition make for a descent down steep scree-runs and boulderfields, aiming directly for the hotel. The descent is incredibly tough and loose, requiring skill and concentration in order to maintain speed. Other runners opt to return by the outward route. Further down, the race crosses heather and bog. There is some debate about the quickest route to the finish, with some runners returning to the gate and along the road, and others making a beeline for the hotel over more heather. Either way, on crossing back over the bridge, runners spirits are lifted as spectators cheer them to the finish. A pint and meal are enjoyed at the prizegiving in the Seumas Bar, where later in the evening the hotel puts on a lively ceilidh.

In 1899, Gurkha Harkbir, companion to pioneer climber Norman Collie, recorded a time of 55 minutes up and down Glamaig – in bare feet! To celebrate this, the Sligachan Hotel owners and Carnethy hill runner David Shepherd devised a plan to organise a race up the hill. Shortly before the first race was due to be held, David tragically died in an accident and hence the race is named in his memory.

◀ Heading up the notorious screes (pic: Anne Nimmo)

Clisham and Mulla-Fo-Dheas

Distance 8km **Ascent** 800m **Time** allow 1h30 **Map** OS Landranger 14

With more descent than ascent, this is a delight for downhill runners. As Clisham in North Harris is the highest peak in the Outer Hebrides, superb all-round views can be savoured from its summit on clear days.

Although the main parking areas for access to Clisham are found along sections of old road east of the highest point on the A859, there are a few smaller parking spots to the west. As this route begins and finishes at different locations, another car or bike should ideally be left at Bun Abhainn Eadarra for the return back up the road. Above Loch a'Mhorghain and along the eastern side of a fence, a route can be picked out bearing northwards up steep tussocky ground and through heather. The ground gradually levels

out and grass cover with occasional wet bog gives pleasant terrain to run over. Ahead the ground rises as Clisham's southern shoulder curves slightly eastwards and becomes strewn with boulders. Some short sections on grass can be found, but inevitably effort will be required to leap over rocks and across boulderfields. The ascent steepens and a path will be found to follow between the rocks to the summit crest, which rests above a substantial drop to the north. After twisting between or bounding over the summit's rocky slabs, the huge cairn encircling the trig point is reached. Clisham's height and commanding position give vast views from the summit on clear days. Head north for a bit, then descend westwards,

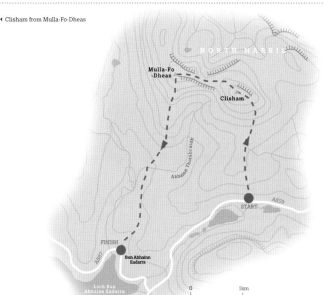

◄ Clisham from Mulla-Fo-Dheas

dropping down sections of grass through the rocks and boulderfields. Pick up a path to cross the narrow bealach and climb a minor bump. Ahead, a steep direct line up the east ridge of Mulla-Fo-Dheas will allow for some easy scrambling. The path, however, turns slightly to the right of the crest on a more gradual incline, eventually approaching the summit from the north. Descending south over boulders, rocks and grass, terrain becomes more runnable as height is quickly lost. Heather is bounded over lower down to reach the Abhainn Thorabraidh, where a rough path is met to follow south to Bun Abhainn Eadarra.

It's hard to imagine commercial whaling taking place in Scotland, but in 1904 on the shore of Loch Bun Abhainn Eadarra, a whaling station was established to process carcasses into fertiliser and feed for livestock. After a chequered life, the station finally ceased operating in 1950 and all that now remains is the tall red-brick chimney and some concrete platforms.

Goatfell Hill Race

Distance 15km Ascent 890m Category AM Records 1:13:40 – Andy Peace (1994), 1:26:21 – Angela Mudge (2001) Time of year mid-May Map OS Landranger 69 Website www.racentries.com

An ascent of Arran's highest peak by the tourist route in a well-organised race. Care is still needed on the descent, however, since injuries are not unknown – as this author can personally testify!

The Ormidale sports fields at the northern end of Brodick is the start location for this fine hill race. The race begins with a lap around the running track, which spreads out the field of runners before they travel out onto the main road. Police hold up the traffic as contestants endure a 1km road race to the bridge over Glenrosa Water. Runners are then directed into Brodick Castle grounds, where they run up a private road along an avenue of beech hedging. The road turns sharply right, beyond which runners are guided onto a track heading into forest. The track climbs uphill and, at a dip, a post marks the start of the main Goatfell path. The incline is gentle and runnable as the path meanders

through birch forest and across burns. As it leaves the forest, the going becomes rougher, crossing granite rocks. Gradually, the path turns west, the ascent steepens and progress becomes more technical as the summit is approached. A short scramble is required up one last incline, beyond which a grassy run reaches Goatfell's summit trig point. Competitors run around the top, then begin the descent back the same way, taking care not to bump into other runners still climbing uphill. Although the view on the return is superb, runners must concentrate on their footwork as the rough granite is unforgiving if rubbed against or fallen onto. After a run back along the road, the race finishes with a sprint around the running track to the sports hall where tea, soup and sandwiches await.

◄ Descending Goatfell's slabs (pic: Keith Burns)

173

Beinn na Caillich horseshoe

Distance 7.5km Ascent 975m Time allow 1h45
Map Harvey Superwalker Skye The Cuillin

Back on Skye, outside Broadford, a classic horseshoe of Beinn na Caillich gives great views, fine ridge running and an exhilarating scree run which counters some of the early effort over heather and boulders to get there.

On the main A87, 1km northwest of Broadford, a sign points to Old Corry. Drive to the end of this road, where there is limited parking just to the north of the turning circle by a bridge over the Allt a'Choire. From the turning circle, cross wet heather and moss-covered ground for 1km, gaining 150m in height. Gradually,

turn northwest and trudge up steeper ground, with the heather replaced by boulders, though never difficult. Grass becomes more widespread as the summit of Beinn na Caillich is approached. A huge cairn and trig point sit on the flat top, with far-reaching views. Now on a path aiming southwest, then west, the terrain is enjoyably runnable down to a bealach. The path becomes more defined as height is gained on the ascent of Beinn Dearg Mhor. Care is needed as the path

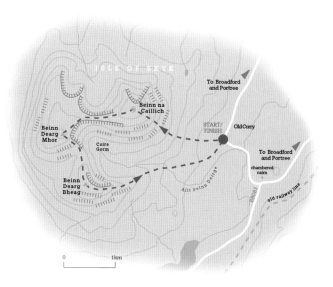

does briefly hug the top of Coire Gorm with its sheer drop just a little too close. Leaving Beinn Dearg Mhor behind and descending southeast, fine scree and gravel can be quickly run down – great fun – you'll want to go back up and do it again, but faster! Climb south up to Beinn Dearg Bheag, where the heather and boulder terrain resembles Perthshire more than Skye. A path twists and turns between the rocks and down through the heather to disappear into wet ground approaching the Allt Beinn Deirge. Cross the burn and bound back over heather to the turning circle.

An alternative start is from the chambered cairn, on the B8083 southwest of Broadford to Torrin and Elgol. This adds an additional 2km on fine track to the route. Near the chambered cairn, a path contours the hillside to the east – this is the remains of a railway set up in the early 20th century to move the then much-in-demand Skye Marble to the pier in Broadford. The railway lasted only a few years before the company went into liquidation and the track was removed.

◀ Beinn na Caillich horseshoe from the chambered cairn

Dun da Ghaoithe

Distance **12km** Ascent 850m Time **allow 2h** Map OS Landranger 49

A track heading to masts on Mainnir nam Fiadh's eastern shoulder makes for a straightforward and very runnable ascent of Mull's only Corbett.

The route begins by the A849, 2km south of the Craignure ferry terminal, where a sign marks the track to the Birds of Prey Centre. Roadside parking near the entrance is not possible, but, with permission, you could park up the track or at the centre. Run up the track past the centre towards forestry. As the track leaves the forest behind, the ascent steepens, but still at a runnable gradient. A mast is reached, then on a more gentle incline, a second mast is met. The track ends at this point and a faint path takes over. This crosses grassy ground and follows the crest of Mainnir nam Fiadh's eastern shoulder, rising and falling over some minor tops. After gaining Mainnir nam Fiadh's summit, bear northwest, running along a wide plateau to reach Dun da Ghaoithe's

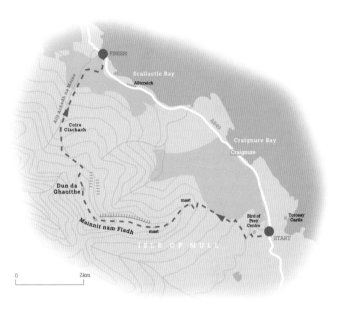

summit with its fine views in all directions. The easiest return is by the same route. However, if transport can be arranged, a fine run can be enjoyed which descends to Scallastle Bay, a scenic bay overlooking the Sound of Mull whose shipwrecks make it a popular diving spot. For this alternative route, head north from Dun da Ghaoithe's summit and drop into Coire

Clachach. Grass, heather and rush is bounded over to reach the Allt Achadh na Moine, which you then shadow down to the forest. With tree stumps hiding in the rush, the terrain becomes briefly troublesome, but a forest track is quickly picked up and followed eastwards to eventually reach the road west of Alltcreich by Scallastle Bay.

◀ Dun da Ghaoithe from the Sound of Mull

Mull Monsterette

Distance 14km Ascent 1500m Category AM Records 1:46:02 – Brian Marshall (2008), 2:03:57 – Jill Mykura (2008) Time of year July Map OS Landranger 48 Website www.carnethy.com

Taking place every two years, the Mull Monsterette is a real challenge of a race, with great, runnable terrain, scree runs, rocky scrambles and fine views. Good head for heights a must.

The race begins at Fada Bridge, which crosses the Abhainn na h-Uamha by Loch na Keal. Runners start off with a flat road run heading northeast on the B8035. After crossing the bridge over the Scarisdale River, competitors turn east on a faint trod through the grass and soft rush. The route begins to

climb and the path has trouble cutting a way through the thickening heather. As the river is left behind, the ascent steepens with a few rocks and boulders to run around and over. On reaching Beinn a'Ghraig's western top, the terrain becomes more runnable heading across the plateau towards the main summit. The crest is now scree covered, but paths heading southeast beyond the summit can be picked up to aid progress down to the bealach before Beinn nan Gabhar. On pathless grass and through rush, runners contour

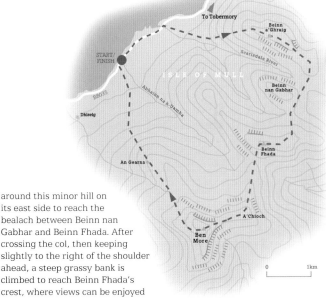

around this minor hill on its east side to reach the bealach between Beinn nan Gabhar and Beinn Fhada. After crossing the col, then keeping slightly to the right of the shoulder ahead, a steep grassy bank is climbed to reach Beinn Fhada's crest, where views can be enjoyed while running to the summit. From there, the descent is initially southwest on scree and boulders to reach another col, this time below A'Chioch. A path is followed uphill and, further on, continues along the narrow ridge, rising steeply on loose ground. Ben More can be seen ahead, with a path making an obvious route across rocky ground. After crossing to the base of the climb and zigzagging up the path, runners climb a steep, rocky section. This is loose, and care is required on the

scramble up. Beyond the top of this awkward section, the path runs to Ben More's summit, where competitors can take an easy option of running down the tourist path to Dhiseig and returning along the road to the finish. Alternatively, after descending 100m on the tourist path, there's a slightly faster but tougher return across scree and wet, grass-covered ground, heading over An Gearna and aiming directly for the finish.

◀ Runners climbing up Ben More's steep rocky section (pic: Willie Gison)

179

Trotternish

Distance 27.5km Ascent 2150m Time allow 4h15 Map Harvey Superwalker
Skye Storr & Trotternish

Starting at the wonderfully weird Old
Man of Storr, this very runnable high-
level route follows a spine of hills and
cliffs to finish on the Quiraing with its
curious features, The Prison, The
Needle and The Table.

This point-to-point route requires
an additional car or a bike to be left
at Bealach Ollasgairte, the high point
on the road between Staffin and Uig.
Start from The Storr car park, 10km
north of Portree on the A855 and

climb through forest to come out just below the base of the Old Man of Storr, a 48m-high needle of rock. On a path, bear north (quite why there is a warning-sign stating 'You are advised not to go beyond this point' is beyond me!) and around the base of The Storr cliffs. The path crosses a fence with barbed wire: follow it for around 50m, then on a fainter path strike SSW directly uphill over grass and occasional scree and rock. There are cliffs above and ahead, but there is a small break which can be scrambled up. The Storr's trig point sits on a grassy top. From here onwards, the terrain is very runnable

and the route more or less follows the cliff edges. Views are stunning along the entire journey. All the named bealachs on the traverse offer escape routes in bad weather. Leave The Storr and drop northwest down grassy ground, then climb uphill, picking up the cliff edge to reach Hartaval. Follow the cliff edge for another 200m, then leave it and jog northwest down to Bealach Hartaval. Pick up the cliff edge and aim north to Sgurr a'Mhalaidh, then the higher

181

summit of Baca Ruadh, beyond which the route turns northwest over Creag a'Lain to Bealach Leacaich with a fence and wall crossing it. More grassy terrain is crossed, following cliffs to reach Beinn Edra, with its trig point and superb views of the Quiraing. Drop NNW on grassy terrain to Bealach Uige, then climb up gentle slopes to Biodha Buidhe. The car park at Bealach Ollasgairte (with snack bar) is just over 1km ahead on a well-defined path. Cross the road, follow the main path for a few metres, then leave it and aim directly uphill on a fainter path. This path travels northeast above the cliffs to reach the top of the Quiraing, where you can peer down into the Prison and to The Table. The summit of Meall na Suiramach is worth reaching to gain uninterrupted views out to the Outer Hebrides. Following the cliff edge, head north for 1km to where a stile crosses a fence; climb over this and on a very obvious path return around the base of the Quiraing to Bealach Ollasgairte.

Isle of Jura Fell Race

Distance **26km** Ascent **2350m** Category **AL** Records **3:06:59 – Mark Rigby (1994)**, **3:40:33 – Angela Mudge (2008)** Time of year **late May** Map **OS Landranger 61** Website **www.jurafellrace.org.uk**

This spirited weekend event on one of the wildest and emptiest of the Inner Hebridean islands is a classic test of hill-running technique and, in mist, navigation skills.

Starting from the distillery in Craighouse, runners head up a track to a communications mast above the village. Leaving the track behind, a faint path is taken over wet ground by the edge of a forest. Onto open hillside, the route crosses wet grass, soft rush and heather to reach the minor bump of Dubh Chreag and continues to Dubh Bheinn. An indistinct trod can be picked up to bear northeast down to some lochans, where in

mist the line of the hill will tempt runners to continue northeast. Instead, keep northwards until another lochan is found, cross the bealach and climb up more grass, heather and occasional rocks to Glas Bheinn. Northwest next, pass a lochan just beyond the summit and continue down along the crest to Aonach Bheinn. The route turns northwards and a fast descent is enjoyed, running down rough heathery steep ground into Gleann Astaile. Once past the Abhainn Gleann Astaile, the easiest route up Beinn a'Chaolais begins up a green bank heading through the boulderfields and heather. Further

◀ The Trotternish Ridge from above Bealach Ollasgairte

Approaching Three Arch Bridge (pic: Andy Spenceley) ▶

up, runners make a gradual turn slightly to the left, hit some boulders and make their way to the flat-topped summit of Beinn a'Chaolais. After turning initially ENE to avoid some crags, the route aims northeast down boulders to a col. Runners then have to work their way up Beinn an Oir using occasional grass and heather sections to avoid a continual ascent up steep scree. Beinn an Oir is the only Corbett on Jura and can catch out runners with its small dark corrie just before the summit. From

the trig point, bear northeast and pass two ruins, then turn ESE and drop down steep heathery and bouldery ground to the bealach below. Climbing directly up the hill ahead, runners work their way up more scree and heather to Beinn Shiantaidh's summit. Beinn Shiantaidh has some surprises and can catch out weary runners – to the northeast of the summit are crags and to the southeast, particularly in mist, scree runs will take tiring runners off bearing and much lower than needed. After descending to the Tana lochans, the route picks up a faint path rising uphill through heather to the last summit, Corra Bheinn. Competitors about-turn and run back down the path to wet grassy ground below. Further on, another wet path aiming directly for Three Arch Bridge can be picked up and followed, crossing Corran River on the way. At Three Arch Bridge, some runners have been known to change from fell shoes to trainers for the 5km flat road run that awaits for the return along the coast to the distillery.

Supported by the Isle of Jura Distillery, the Jura Fell Race is an event not to be missed in the hill race calendar. Runners' tents take over the grass in front of the hotel, friends catch up in the pub and restaurant and a ceilidh is held in the evening after the race. A number of prizes are awarded after the race, but the most coveted is the small engraved whisky glass given to the few runners who manage to complete the course in under four hours. Everyone, however, is awarded a Jura Fell Race T-shirt!

Index of hills

Munros: Hills and mountains over 3000 feet
Corbetts: Hills over 2500 feet and less than 3000 feet
Grahams: Hills over 2000 feet and less than 2500 feet
Donalds: Hills over 2000 feet in the Scottish Lowlands (so includes some Grahams)
Others: Other significant hills mentioned in the text

Corbetts

Grahams

Index of hills

Race calendar

January

February

March

April

May

June

July

August

September

October

November

Running record

Run	Date	Time

Run   Date   Time

Run	Date	Time